指导单位

上海市文物局

百物看中国
CHINA 100
OUTBOUND EXHIBITION SERIES OF ARTS AND CULTURES
文|物|艺|术|出|境|大|展|系|列

上海博物馆"百物看中国"文物艺术出境大展系列
CHINA 100: Outbound Exhibition Series of Arts and Cultures

中国汉代文物精品

THE JADE AMOUR OF IMMORTALITY
TREASURES OF HAN PERIOD CHINA

不朽的玉甲

上海博物馆
Shanghai Museum

上海书画出版社

总　序

　　求木之长者，必固其根本；欲流之远者，必浚其泉源。

　　习近平总书记指出，中华优秀传统文化是中华文明的智慧结晶和精华所在，是中华民族的根和魂，是我们在世界文化激荡中站稳脚跟的根基。中国理应同世界各地遵循相互尊重和平等互利的原则，以对话增进互信，以合作实现共赢，以交流筑牢友谊。

　　国际博物馆协会关于"博物馆"的最新定义强调：博物馆具有可及性和包容性，促进多样性和可持续性，为教育、欣赏、深思和知识共享提供多种体验。目前，中国共备案博物馆六千余座，正积极发挥保护和传承人类文明重要殿堂的作用，努力搭建起连接过去、现在和未来的桥梁，让人们深刻体悟到中华文明的博大精深、源远流长，并促进各国人民相互理解与信任，推动不同文明在交流互鉴中共同进步、繁荣发展。

　　作为世界顶级的中国古代艺术博物馆，上海博物馆在建馆 70 周年再出发的进程中，着眼"以物论史、以史增信"，聚焦"建设大场馆、引领大科创、配置大资源、打造大品牌"，提出并实施"大博物馆计划"。通过做强"何以中国""对话世界""百物看中国"三大系列展览品牌，构建"3+X"新发展格局即以上海博物馆人民广场馆、东馆、北馆为核心，在海内外设立若干上海博物馆展厅或分馆，全力打造具有世界影响力，具有中国特色、中国风格、中国气派的博物馆文化品牌。

　　"百物看中国"文物艺术出境大展系列是上海博物馆"大博物馆计划"的重要组成部分。该大展系列将依托丰富的馆藏文物，并强化国内顶级文博机构优质资源配置，着力打造上海博物馆"中华文化走出去"的"始发港"和"金名片"，演绎上海精彩，讲好中国故事，传播中国声音，展现可信、可爱、可敬的中国形象。我们相信，这正是上海博物馆界对习近平总书记提出"全球文明倡议"的生动实践，亦是构建人类命运共同体的应有之义。

　　从百物看中国，方寸之间览千年，中华文明浩瀚如海，姹紫嫣红齐绽放。

　　从中国看百物，沧海之间观一粟，华夏历史盈千累万，百花千卉共芬芳。

上海市文化和旅游局　上海市文物局

局长

2023 年 4 月

Foreword

"If a tree wants to grow tall, the root needs nourishing; if a river wants to run afar, the origin needs unblocking."

— *Ten Pieces of Advice to the Taizong Emperor*, Wei Zheng (580–643)

As indicated by Xi Jinping, the General Secretary of Communist Party of China (CPC), the highlights of traditional Chinese culture reflect the wisdom of Chinese civilization as well as the heart and soul of all ethnic groups in China, serving as the solid ground upon which the Chinese encounter global cultural vicissitudes. We are thus required, in the world stage, to uphold the principle of respecting each other based on equality for the sake of mutual benefits. We should enhance mutual understanding in dialogues, reach win-win scenario in cooperation and deepen friendship in communication.

The International Council of Museums (ICOM), in its latest museum definition, points out that "[…] accessible and inclusive, museums foster diversity and sustainability, […] offering varied experiences for education, enjoyment, reflection and knowledge sharing." Now there are over 6,000 museums registered in China. Open to the public, they are the centers who conserve and interpret human civilizations, build a bridge between the past, present and future, enable the audience to deeply understand profundity and dynamics of Chinese civilization, promote understanding and trust between people in different nations as well as progress and prosperity in various cultures via exchange of ideas.

As a world-class hub for ancient Chinese art, the Shanghai Museum, just turning 70-year-old last year, repivots based on the principle of encouraging self-confidence through researching history and heritage with substantial materials. Envisioning a better future for the venues, academics, exhibitions and services, the Museum has launched the Greater Museum Complex Program, which includes three exhibition series, *The Essence of China*, *A Dialogue with the World*, and *CHINA 100*; developing "3+X" structure that combines venues of the Museum in People's Square, the under-construction east building in Pudong, the future north building on Yangpu riverside as well as more branches of the Museum in China and abroad. In a nutshell, the Museum is sparing no effort to becoming a global influencer on promoting Chinese culture with Chinese characteristics.

CHINA 100: Outbound Exhibition Series of Arts and Cultures plays an important role in the Program. The series is initiated based on the collections of the Museum, which will be supported by cooperation with other top-class national cultural institutions. Thus, the series is being built up to become the port-of-departure for the voyage of Chinese culture in the world; a recognizable name card of Chinese culture. The series, as an organic part of the global civilization initiative and community of common destiny for mankind, is ready to show the world the glamour of Shanghai and present a China that is credible, appealing and respectable.

To sum up, *CHINA 100* is an exhibition series that offers a window for the global audience to learn about the profound and multi-faceted Chinese civilization. Yet, the history of Chinese culture lies in a broader spectrum where different elements play their own distinctive roles.

FANG Shizhong　Director-General
Shanghai Municipal Administration of Culture and Tourism
Shanghai Municipal Administration of Cultural Heritage
April, 2023

致　辞

　　汉朝国力强盛、经济繁荣、文化昌明，成为傲居东方的强大国家，与欧亚大陆彼端的罗马帝国遥相辉映。汉朝时期，中国的政治、经济、文化、艺术、军事、科技等各个方面都取得了长足的进步和发展。丝绸之路的开辟，更架起了中国与周边国家之间经济文化交流的桥梁。这些成就不仅为后世留下了丰厚的遗产，也为世界文明的发展做出了重要的贡献。"汉语""汉字""汉族""汉文化"等词沿用至今，皆是汉朝在中国文化乃至世界文明中留下的深刻印记，成为了中华文明绵延数千年赓续不断的象征。

　　此次"不朽的玉甲——中国汉代文物精品"展的展品主要来自上海博物馆、徐州博物馆和成都文物考古研究院。逾百件出土及传世文物奇珍，或栩栩如生，或精美细腻，或古朴神秘，旨在多角度、多层次揭示汉朝历史、文化和艺术风貌，探讨中华文明的文脉传承与中西方文化交流历史。

　　此次展览作为上海博物馆"百物看中国"文物艺术出境大展系列首展，第一站来到匈牙利，具有深远的意义。2023年正值"一带一路"倡议提出十周年，匈牙利是第一个与中国共建"一带一路"的欧洲国家，与中国友谊深厚，两国人文交流密切。我们很荣幸能有此次机会，同莫拉·弗朗茨博物馆合作，与匈牙利及欧洲观众分享我们的馆藏，重现中国历史中的这段华彩篇章。

　　在此，衷心感谢匈牙利莫拉·弗朗茨博物馆、佰路得信息技术（上海）有限公司，以及徐州博物馆和成都文物考古研究院等各方机构同仁合力共同促成此次展览。希望以此次展览为契机，开拓未来中匈两国文博机构更广泛、更深入的合作，更好地促进两国之间的文明互鉴与民心相通。

上海博物馆馆长

Message

    Han was a powerful and prosperous dynasty with a thriving economy and flourishing cultures, a strong power in the East that paralleled the Roman Empire on the other side of the Eurasian continent. The Han dynasty saw remarkable progress and development in politics, economy, culture, art, military, technology, and other fields. The Silk Road established during the Han dynasty opened a bridge fundamental for economic and cultural exchanges between China and neighbouring countries. These achievements not only left a rich legacy for future Chinese dynasties but also contributed significantly to the development of world civilisations. Words such as *Hanyu* (Chinese language), *Hanzi* (Chinese characters), *Hanzu* (Han ethnic group), and *Hanwenhua* (Han culture) are still in use today, which are snapshots of the dynasty's profound imprints on Chinese and world cultures, reflecting the honourable continuity of Chinese civilisation through thousands of years.

    The major exhibits of the exhibition *The Jade Armour of Immortality – Treasures of Han Period China* consist of more than a hundred pieces of cultural relics from the collections of the Shanghai Museum, the Xuzhou Museum, and the Chengdu Institute of Archaeology. Vividly lifelike, exquisitely delicate, or marvellously mysterious – the treasures provide glimpses into the history, culture, and art of the Han dynasty from diverse perspectives and explore the exchange history of China with the West.

    As the first of *CHINA 100: Outbound Exhibition Series of Arts and Cultures* of the Shanghai Museum, the exhibition taking place in Hungary is of great significance. 2023 marks the 10th anniversary of China's Belt and Road initiative, in which Hungary is the first European country to join. The two countries have traditionally enjoyed genuine friendship and intense cultural exchanges. We are honoured to have this opportunity to collaborate with the Móra Ferenc Museum and present our collections from one of the most brilliant chapters in Chinese history to Hungarian and European audiences.

    We would like to express our heartfelt thanks to the Móra Ferenc Museum, Back & Rosta Kft., and colleagues from the Xuzhou Museum and the Chengdu Institute of Archaeology, who have worked together to make this exhibition possible. We hope that this exhibition will be a start for more extensive and in-depth collaborations between Chinese and Hungarian museums in the future to better promote cultural connections and mutual understanding between our countries.

CHU Xiaobo   Director
Shanghai Museum

前　言

　　2023年是"一带一路"倡议提出十周年。为了深入贯彻落实习近平总书记关于推动文明交流互鉴的重要论述精神，在上海博物馆的牵头推动下，上海博物馆、徐州博物馆和成都文物考古研究院联合举办的"不朽的玉甲——中国汉代文物精品"展于2023年6月24日在匈牙利塞格德莫拉·弗朗茨博物馆隆重开展，这对于进一步增进中匈人民友谊、加强文明交流互鉴、助力"一带一路"建设都具有重要意义。

　　徐州，古称彭城，自古为华夏九州之一。徐州拥有五千多年的文明史和两千六百多年的建城史，是彭祖古国、刘邦故里、项羽故都。特别是两汉四百年间，先后有十三位楚王、五位彭城王定都彭城，徐州市区周围已发现、发掘西汉楚王（后）墓八处十九座、东汉彭城王（后）墓两处五座，以及包括刘氏宗室在内的中小型墓葬近四千座。徐州汉墓、汉画像石、汉兵马俑为代表的"汉代三绝"，形成了"两汉文化看徐州"的核心。

　　《说文解字》言："玉，石之美，有五德，润泽以温，仁之方也，鰓理自外，可以知申，义之方也，其声舒扬，专以远闻，智之方也，不能而折，勇之方也，锐察而不恔，洁之方玉也。"汉代玉器是徐州博物馆藏品中的翘楚，一是数量多，仅狮子山楚王墓就出土近两百件；二是品类全，礼仪、装饰、生活、丧葬类玉器都极其精美；三是玉质佳，除葬玉外，出土玉器多数为透闪石质，以白玉、青白玉为主，晶莹温润，质地细腻，如玉卮、龙凤纹玉璜、S形龙佩、玉剑饰、玉熊等；四是葬玉丰富，镶玉漆棺、玉衣、玉面罩、玉枕、玉握、玉九窍塞等数量众多，形制多样。目前徐州地区已经出土的完、残玉衣有十五件，修复展出的有狮子山楚王墓金缕玉衣、火山刘和墓银缕玉衣、拉犁山东汉墓铜缕玉衣，其中刘和墓银缕玉衣没有被盗扰，也是全国仅有的两件完整的银缕玉衣之一。此次展览，徐州博物馆精心选备了1995年出土于徐州狮子山楚王墓的S形玉龙佩、虎头玉枕饰、双联玉管，1991年出土于徐州市后楼山汉墓的西汉缀玉面饰，1996年出土于徐州九里区火山刘和墓的玉握、西汉木芯镶玉贴金（箔）枕等十八件（套）汉代玉器文物参展，所展玉器基本代表了徐州汉代文物的顶尖水平。

　　习近平总书记强调"中华优秀传统文化是中华民族的精神命脉，是涵养社会主义核心价值观的重要源泉，也是我们在世界文化激荡中站稳脚跟的坚实根基"。衷心地希望能够通过本次展览构筑起巩固中匈人民友谊的桥梁，引导更多匈牙利人民深入了解中国玉器文化；同时在推动中华优秀传统文化创造性转化和创新性发展以及践行习近平文化思想、建设中华民族现代文明的进程中作出新的更大贡献。

徐州博物馆馆长

Message

2023 marks the tenth anniversary of the Belt and Road initiative. In alignment with the principles of cultural exchange and mutual learning emphasized by President Xi Jinping, *The Jade Armour of Immortality – Treasures of Han Period China*, co-hosted by the Shanghai Museum, Xuzhou Museum, and Chengdu Institute of Archaeology opened on 24 June 2023 at the Móra Ferenc Museum in Szeged, Hungary. This exhibition holds significance for further enhancing the friendship between the Chinese and Hungarian peoples, strengthening cultural exchange and mutual learning, and contributing to the development of the Belt and Road initiative.

Xuzhou, known as Pengcheng in ancient times, boasts a civilization that spans over 5000 years and has held city status for over 2600 years. It is where the ancient state of Peng was located during the Shang dynasty, the hometown of Liu Bang (Emperor Gaozu of Han, 256–195 BCE), and the capital of the Western Chu ruled by Xiang Yu (c. 232–202 BCE). Thirteen Chu Kings of the Western Han and five Pengcheng Kings of the Eastern Han made the city their capital. In the vicinity of Xuzhou have been discovered eight sites and nineteen tombs of Chu kings and queens, as well as two sites and five tombs of Pengcheng kings and queens. Nearly 4000 small to medium-sized tombs, including those of the Liu family, have also been found. Among the findings, the "Three Marvels of the Han Dynasty" – tombs, stone reliefs, and terracotta warriors – are the pillars of Xuzhou's pivotal role in representing the Han dynasty culture.

According to *Shuowen Jiezi* (*An Explication of Written Characters*), jade is a type of beautiful stone that possesses five virtues – benevolence, righteousness, wisdom, courage, and purity. The Han dynasty jade artefacts crown the Xuzhou Museum's collection. Those excavated from the tombs of Chu kings at Shizishan alone number almost 200 pieces. The extensive categories cover exquisite jades for rituals, decoration, daily use, and burials. Apart from burial jades, most excavated pieces are made of translucent serpentine in white and greenish-white colours, with clear, mild finish and fine texture, as shown in exemplars of jade vessels, *huang*-pedants with dragon-phoenix pattern, S-shaped dragon pendants, sword fittings, and bear figurines. The diversity of burial jades is demonstrated by a large and varied collection of jade-inlaid lacquer coffins, jade suites, face coverings, headrests, grips, and orifices fittings. Currently, fifteen jade suits have been unearthed in Xuzhou, among which the gold-threaded jade suit from the Chu King's tomb at Shizishan, the silver-threaded suit from Liuhe's tomb at Huoshan, and the copper-threaded suit from the Eastern Han tomb at Lalishan are on display after restoration. The suit from Liuhe's tomb has not been looted and is one of the only two intact silver-threaded jade suits in China. For this exhibition, the Xuzhou Museum has selected eighteen pieces/sets of Han dynasty jade artefacts, including the S-shaped dragon pendant, tiger-head-shaped headrest ornament, and paired tubes unearthed from the Chu King's tomb at Shizishan in 1995; the face covering unearthed from the Han tomb at Houloushan in 1991; and the jade grip and jade-inlaid wood headrest with gold foil unearthed from Liuhe's tomb at Huoshan in 1996. These artefacts exemplify the pinnacle of Xuzhou's Han dynasty heritage.

President Xi Jinping emphasized that the outstanding traditional culture of China is the spiritual backbone of the Chinese nation, an important source of nurturing the core values of socialism, and a solid foundation for us to stand firm among world cultures. We sincerely hope that this exhibition can build a bridge to strengthen the friendship between the Chinese and Hungarian peoples, inviting more Hungarian audience to learn Chinese jade culture, and make new and greater contributions to promoting the creative transformation and innovative development of China's traditional culture, implementing Xi's theories, and building the modern civilization of the Chinese nation.

LI Xiaojun　Director
Xuzhou Museum

前　言

　　"蚕丛及鱼凫，开国何茫然"，长期以来，人们总是难以将成都平原悠远而漫长的古蜀时期从传说和想象中完全分离出来。随着 20 世纪 80 年代以来广汉三星堆遗址、成都金沙遗址、成都十二桥遗址以及以新津宝墩遗址为代表的八大史前古城址等一系列新石器时代晚期至夏商周时期遗存被发现，神话时代的历史脉络开始凸显，古蜀文明的神秘面目逐渐清晰。

　　公元前 316 年，秦并蜀，这是中国历史发展进程中一次重要事件。此后，秦灭六国，实现大一统，为今后中国历史的发展奠定了坚实的基础。蜀地自然条件优越，秦在此开展移民拓地、修筑城池、兴建水利等一系列治理措施，逐渐将其变为"水旱从人，不知饥谨"的天府之国。至汉代时成都已发展成为全国五大城市之一，经济、文化、商贸、教育等众多领域都处于全国领先地位。

　　汉代成都织锦业繁荣，中央政府遂在此设立锦官管理，因此成都又称"锦官城"。成都漆器工艺战国时已经十分精湛，汉代时产品远近闻名，带有"蜀郡西工造"字样的漆器甚至在今朝鲜半岛和蒙古高原都有发现。景帝末年，蜀郡太守文翁在成都创立中国最早的地方官学——文翁石室，开启了成都崇文重教的传统，"学徒鳞萃，蜀学比于齐鲁"，成都成为比肩孔孟之乡的文化教育中心。作为南方丝绸之路西道的起点，成都与周边国家和地区的文化交流早在古蜀时期就已经产生。汉代张骞出使西域，就曾在大宛（今乌兹别克斯坦）、大夏（今阿富汗）见到从身毒（今印度）贩运来的蜀布和邛竹杖。

　　近年来，成都地区两汉考古工作取得了丰富成果，出土了以天府汉碑、天回医简、经络俑、提花织机、铜车马、说唱俑、画像石、画像砖、玉器等为代表的一大批丰富且精美的文物，加之难以计数的日用陶器、模型、陶俑等，构建出一幅"百伎千工，东西鳞集，南北并凑，驰逐相逢，周流往来"的生动汉代社会图景。

　　2023 年是共建"一带一路"倡议提出十周年，本次展览汇集了中国汉代出土的各类代表性文物，旨在激发海内外观众对中国古代文化的兴趣，进一步加深了解、增进交流。成都文物考古研究院本次参展的漆陶鼎、俳优俑、吹笛俑、胡人面具、陶狗、双阙画像砖等均是成都乃至四川地区汉代文物的代表，是当时成都社会繁华富庶、人民乐观包容、文化创新交流的一个缩影，代表了古代成都张开双手、拥抱世界的广阔胸襟，也体现了现代成都增进文明交流互鉴、促进共同发展的积极尝试。

成都文物考古研究院院长

颜劲松

Message

As Tang dynasty poet Li Bai (701–762) wrote in his poem, "The ancient rulers founded and developed Shu a long time ago, all the history is so distant and hard to trace now", the history of Ancient Shu based on the Chengdu Plain once had long been discerned only in legends and imagination. However, since the 1980s, the discovery of late Neolithic to Xia-Shang-Zhou period remnants, such as the Sanxingdui site in Guanghan, Jinsha site and Shierqiao site in Chengdu, and the eight prehistoric ancient city sites represented by the Baodun site in Xinjin, has gradually unveiled the history of the mythical era before the Xia dynasty and the mystery of Ancient Shu civilization.

In 316 BCE, Qin conquered Shu, marking a pivotal event in China's history. Later, Qin unified the country, laying a solid foundation for the future development of China. Endowed with favourable natural conditions, the Shu region allowed Qin to unfold immigration, city construction, water conservancy, and other measures that gradually transformed the region into the "Land of Plenty" where people harnessed natural resources and lived without knowing famine. By the Han dynasty, Chengdu had evolved into one of the five major cities in the country, taking a leading position in economy, culture, trade, and education.

Chengdu's brocade weaving industry thrived in the Han dynasty, leading to the establishment of the Brocade Bureau by the central government. This earned Chengdu the moniker "The City of Brocade Bureau". Additionally, lacquerware craftsmanship, refined since the Warring States period, gained widespread fame during the Han dynasty. Lacquerwares with the inscription "Shu Jun Xi Gong Zao (Made by the Western Workshop of Shu Commandery)" have been found even on today's Korean Peninsnla and Mongolian Plateau. In the late years of Emperor Jing's reign (157–141 BCE), the Shu Commandery Governor Wen Weng established China's earliest local official school – *Wenweng Shishi* ("Stone Chamber of Wen Weng") in Chengdu, initiating Chengdu's tradition of valuing culture and education. Having nurtured many outstanding individuals, Chengdu has become a cultural and educational centre comparable to the homeland of Confucius and Mencius. As the starting point of the Southern Silk Road, Chengdu had cultural exchanges with surrounding countries and regions as early as the Ancient Shu period. Han-dynasty diplomat Zhang Qian (c. 164–114 BCE), during his mission to the Western Regions, once encountered cloth and bamboo canes original to Shu that arrived in Dayuan (in present-day Uzbekistan) and Da Xia (in present-day Afghanistan) through India.

Recent archaeological work on Western Han sites in the Chengdu region has yielded abundant results. Among the numerous exquisite treasures unearthed are the Tianfu Stele, Tianhui Medical Bamboo Slips, figurines with meridian-collateral diagrams, looms, bronze chariots and horses, comedian figurines, stone reliefs, relief bricks, and jades, and varied everyday items like earthenware vessels, models, and figurines. Together, they depict a dynamic panorama of Han dynasty society, where artisans excelled, products flowed, cultures met, and people interacted.

As 2023 marks the tenth anniversary of the Belt and Road initiative, this exhibition assembles a diverse array of representative Han dynasty artefacts unearthed in China. It aims to kindle interest in ancient Chinese culture among audiences at home and abroad, fostering deeper understanding and enhanced cultural exchange. The lacquer tripod, comedian figurine, musician figurine, Hu mask, dog model, brick with towers and other objects presented by the Chengdu Institute of Archaeology are emblematic of typical Han dynasty artefacts from Chengdu and Sichuan. They capture the essence of a flourishing and prosperous Chengdu society during that era, characterized by optimistic and inclusive people, as well as innovative cultural exchanges. These artefacts embody the cultural openness of the ancient Chengdu, reflecting the modern city's ongoing efforts to promote cultural exchange and mutual learning, facilitating shared development.

YAN Jinsong　Director
Chengdu Institute of Archaeology

目 录
Contents

古邦丝绸路 犹闻大汉风

走进"不朽的玉甲——中国汉代文物精品"展

褚晓波

　　2023 年，是共建"一带一路"倡议提出十周年。2015 年，匈牙利成为首个加入这一倡议的欧洲国家。2023 年 6 月 24 日，由上海博物馆（以下简称上博）领衔，徐州博物馆、成都文物考古研究院联合举办的"不朽的玉甲——中国汉代文物精品"展，在匈牙利南部城市塞格德的莫拉·弗朗茨博物馆开幕（图 1、2）。这一天，恰逢匈牙利博物馆日，展览开放至午夜 12 点，中华优秀传统文化的魅力深深打动了当日前来参观的近万名观众。展览将延续至 12 月 31 日，随后在多国巡回展出，旨在激发海外受众对中国古代艺术文化的兴趣和了解，增进各国文明的交流互鉴。

图 1 展览开幕式现场　　　　　　　　　　　图 2 展览开幕当天的莫拉·弗朗茨博物馆门前广场

自汉开篇，华章璀璨

　　中华文明历史悠久，蕴涵广博。汉代通常被认为是汉民族意识开始形成的时代，汉帝国则是中国历史上第一个具有世界影响力的帝国，与罗马帝国、贵霜帝国、安息帝国并称古代世界史中的四大帝国。在本次展览中，上博集结工艺研究部、青铜研究部、陶瓷研究部的多名专业人员商讨、研究展陈内容，确定以丝路渐成之时的汉代为主题，分为"敦睦的智慧""生活的艺术""信仰的光芒"三个单元。青铜器、陶器、玉器、漆器、印章、石刻、钱币等百余件文物精品，引领海外观众从西汉启程，穿梭千年光阴，展现出中华文明源远流长、光辉灿烂的历史华章。

　　建汉之初，汉代统治者实行"郡国并行制"。两汉悠悠四百余年，今江苏徐州一带曾属七个不同的诸侯国，历经数十位诸侯王，是汉代中央政府为巩固统治而推行分封制度的集中体现地之一。"敦睦的智慧"单元精选徐州狮子山楚王陵出土的数件玉器文物，其中虎头形玉枕饰为某代楚王玉枕上的附件（图3-1），由新疆和田青白玉精雕而成，晶莹剔透、虎虎生威。这批出土玉器用料精良、工艺卓著，是当时诸侯王权力和地位的写照，也是西汉早期"以镇抚四海，用承卫天子"这一政治制度的缩影。

　　在儒家思想影响下，汉代社会倡导亲善和睦、安居乐业，手工业得到长足发展，器物制作渐重实用，工匠们在饰纹和造型中融入对世界的细致观察与匠心巧思。展览单元"生活的艺术"展出画像砖、画像石、陶壶、陶灯、漆杯、漆奁、铜镜、铜带钩等文物，展现了汉代建筑、器用、妆饰等物品精巧的制作工艺。在器用类文物中，一件西汉漆耳杯上的彩绘鱼纹尤得匈方展陈人员的喜爱（图3-2）。耳杯呈椭圆形，口微敛，弧腹，平底，两侧新月形耳微翘。杯为木胎斫制，内髹朱漆，外部及耳部髹黑漆。内底中央以黑漆细描一鱼，并用深浅不同的黑漆区分髹涂鱼眼、鱼鳞、鱼尾等。鱼身修长，似在水中悠游，生趣盎然。西汉是中国古代漆器发展的高峰时期，饮酒具较食具在当时更受重视，又以漆杯为出土数量最多、使用时间最长的器类之一。考古发现，漆杯常与卮、盘等配套，反映出汉代"百礼之会，非酒不行"的社会风俗。

　　汉代民众对宇宙和未知世界的理解飞扬浪漫，他们想象出天空四象、飞凤游龙和神仙居所，创造了一个逍遥自在、雄奇多彩的信仰世界。"信仰的光芒"单元中的四灵纹胜形玉佩浓缩展现了汉代人的精神世界（图3-3）。佩上浅刻篆书铭文"长宜子孙，延寿万年"，并以透雕手法雕出"天之四灵"，即青龙、白虎、朱雀、玄武四种具有方位意义的灵兽。"四灵"常以较为固定的方阵出现在汉代画像石、壁画、铜镜、陶器等物质载体上，寓意天下大治、人民安居乐业。玉佩所作"胜"形则来自《山海经》中对西王母外貌的描述："豹尾虎齿而善啸，蓬发戴胜。"由于汉代精心经营西域，与"西极"相关的西王母神话流行甚广。有学者认为，汉代民众的西王母信仰或与当时人们对希腊、罗马的懵懂认知相互关联，商人们在丝绸之路"相

图3-1 展品中的西汉虎头形玉枕饰（徐州博物馆藏）　　图3-2 展品中的西汉彩绘鱼纹漆耳杯（上海博物馆藏）　　图3-3 展品中的东汉四灵纹胜形玉佩（上海博物馆藏）

望于道”“相属不绝”，沟通有无的在丝绸、玻璃器、茶叶等商品之外，还有文化艺术的吉光片羽。

东西交融，丝路繁盛

秦汉时期，中国已有通往南海诸国的海上运输线，西汉开始，逐步形成联通西域的陆上运输线。在漫长的历史时空中，横跨海陆、迤逦万里的丝绸之路成为促进亚欧大陆文化交流、文明进步的桥梁，不仅推动了中国与西方国家的商品交易和贸易发展，也促进了东西方文明的交流与融合。

秉持自主策划、共同策展的理念，本次展览特设“丝路的繁盛”单元。匈牙利亚洲艺术研究专家方天娟（吉奥尔基·法伊萨克）参与策划并挑选了莫拉·弗朗茨博物馆馆藏中具有典型匈奴民族特色的铜带饰、铜镯饰、铜吊坠、铜刀等数十件文物，时间涵盖公元前 6 世纪至公元 4 世纪，力图与来自中国的文物共同呈现历史上丝路沿线文明的不同侧面。

虎是匈奴民族最喜欢的动物之一，在艺术品中常有表现，反映出草原民族对强者的崇敬。在这些匈牙利文物中，四件腰带饰的制作年代与中国东周时期相当，为青铜或青铜镀银质地，装饰有“卷曲的掠食者形象”，部分可辨认为老虎咬羊或老虎咬牦牛的图案。这类纹饰图案常被中国学者称为虎噬动物纹，多见于商代晚期至两汉时期，与这批匈牙利腰带饰出土时间相近的代表文物有河北中山国王𰯼墓出土的错金银虎噬鹿纹铜屏风插座（图 4–1）、内蒙古自治区阿鲁柴登墓出土的虎噬动物纹金冠饰和金带饰，以及甘肃省天水市张家川马家塬战国墓出土虎噬羊纹金腰带饰等（图 4–2）。学者认为，这一纹样最早形成于长城地带中段，随欧亚草原游牧民族往来迁徙而传播、影响多地，成为不同地区文明交流互鉴的生动缩影。

图 4–1 河北中山国王𰯼墓出土错金银虎噬鹿纹铜屏风插座

图 4–2 甘肃马家塬战国墓出土虎噬羊纹金腰带饰

图 5 展品中的东汉胡人面具（成都文物考古研究院藏）

本次展览中有一副成都出土的泥质灰陶胡人面具格外引人注目（图 5），时代为东汉晚期，推测为傩舞演员佩戴使用。"胡"是中国古代对北方边地及西域各民族的称呼。张骞凿空西域后，中国与西域多国往来不断，西域胡人亦来到中国西南四川等地。两汉时期的画像石、画像砖、陶俑乃至壁画中有大量胡人形象，他们头戴尖帽，深目高鼻，或奏乐舞蹈，或饮酒献宝，或驯狮牵骆驼等。胡人的到来为汉代艺术带来新鲜的文化因子，例如悠扬婉转的横笛，"十二门前融冷光，二十三丝动紫皇"的箜篌，都成为中原的常见乐器，汉代乐府诗《孔雀东南飞》中便有刘兰芝"十五弹箜篌"的描写，足见当时来自西域的乐器已经进入中原寻常百姓家。

以文化人，大道同行

"不朽的玉甲——中国汉代文物精品"展是上博"百物看中国"文物艺术出境大展系列首展。过去几年间，上博与匈牙利文博机构合作紧密：2017 年，上博举办"茜茜公主与匈牙利：17—19 世纪匈牙利贵族生活"展，通过匈牙利国家博物馆的 149 件馆藏精品，见微知著地展现出匈牙利这段时期的历史和艺术风貌；2019 年，上博与匈牙利中央银行和雅典娜智慧之家基金会共同举办"丝绸之路上的中国和匈牙利：钱币的旅程"展，陈列了公元前 2 世纪至今共 190 枚各具代表性的两国钱币，从丝绸之路上出现的古钱币到当下流行的移动支付，勾勒出货币漫长的发展历程。2023 年，"不朽的玉甲"展成功举办，既是中华文化"走出去"迈出的更坚实一步，也是献给共建"一带一路"倡议十周年盛事的贺礼。

回顾过往，自 1952 年建馆以来，上博已赴世界三十多个国家和地区、九十余座城市，举办了近一百五十场出境展览，累计外展文物超过七千件（套），观众总数超过二千万人次，多层次、多角度地向世界展现了可信、可爱、可敬的中国形象。在策划出境展览时，上博特别注重对于艺术和艺术史的研究呈现，强调自主策划、共同策展，提升与世界博物馆界对话的能力。如，2018 年 3 月，上博与法国塞努奇博物馆共同策办的"中国芳香：中国古代香文化"展在巴黎举行（图 6-1），陶瓷、绘画、青铜，一件件精美器物细致入微地体现香融入中国古人日常生活的点点滴滴。展览将中国香文化和法国香文化并置展出，体现两种香文化的异同，广受海外观众欢迎。

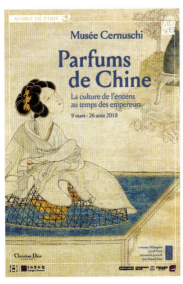

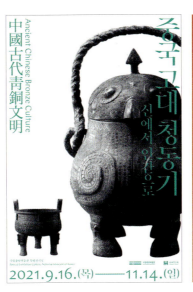

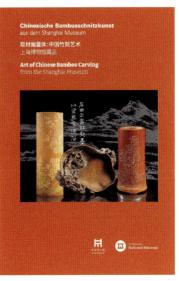

图 6-1 2018 年赴法国"中国芳香 : 中国古代香文化"展　　图 6-2 2021 年赴韩国"中国古代青铜文明"展　　图 6-3 2022 年赴列支敦士登"取材幽篁体——中国竹刻艺术"展

2021 年 9 月，上博在韩国国立中央博物馆举办"中国古代青铜文明"特展（图 6-2），展出馆藏 68 件 (套) 展品，时间跨越一千五百余年，展现了器型多样、造型丰富、纹饰瑰丽的中国古代青铜文明，完整呈现了中国青铜器的发生、发展、演变轨迹，阐释了青铜器的历史、艺术与科技价值，从一个侧面展示出中国文化的深厚积淀，以及对东亚文化圈的深刻影响。2022 年 2 月，由上博自主策划的"取材幽篁体——中国竹刻艺术"展赴列支敦士登国家博物馆展出（图 6-3），遴选的 60 件中国竹刻精品的时代横跨 17 世纪上半叶至 20 世纪中叶，系统展示出中国竹刻艺术的艺术特色与工艺特点。在这些极具中国民族特色的手工艺品引领下，海外观众走进由中国传统工艺与江南文人美学构成的艺术世界，切身感受到中国传统文化的趣味与风雅。

结语

为回应时代之变、中国之进、人民之呼，上博于 2022 年 12 月推出"大博物馆计划"，力争在"十四五"期间建成"中国特色世界一流"博物馆、"一带一路"文明交流全球核心博物馆、世界顶级的中国古代艺术博物馆。力争到 21 世纪中叶打造成为全球艺术的顶级殿堂、国际文博的学术高地、文旅融合的卓越典范、人民城市的重要标识以及文明互鉴的形象大使。展望未来，上博将继续推出聚焦全球文明交流互鉴的"对话世界"文物艺术大展系列，与英国博物馆、英国国家美术馆、法国卢浮宫等世界知名文博机构展开合作，引进高质量海外展览；继续推动与印度尼西亚等国家开展的"海上丝绸之路"考古研究和水下考古调查；继续组织策划上博文化"走出去"品牌——"百物看中国"系列文物艺术出境展。

　　博物馆是保护和传承人类文明的重要殿堂，也是文明交流互鉴的重要平台，通过博物馆推进以文物为载体的交流互鉴，有助于进一步拉紧不同文明之间的人文纽带，促进不同文明民心相通。在这一过程中，上博将主动拓展国际视野、增强国际思维、加强国际对标，建立跨国家、跨学科、跨领域的协同创新机制，讲好中国故事，传播好中国声音，进一步扩大中华文明的传播力和影响力，提升中华文化在全球文化版图中的深度与广度。

Echoes of the Mighty Han: On the *Treasures of Han Period China* Exhibition

CHU Xiaobo

Abstract

Celebrating the 10th anniversary of the Belt and Road initiative, the Shanghai Museum kicked off the *CHINA 100* outbound exhibition series by staging *Treasures of Han Period China* in Szeged, Hungary, in June 2023. Through over 100 pieces/sets of artefacts, the exhibition curated by the Shanghai Museum sheds light on the splendour of the Han dynasty, a golden age in Chinese history, illustrating its profound influence on the identity of the Chinese civilization and the exchanges between East and West ever since. The Han dynasty artefacts, spanning jade, bronze, ceramics, lacquer, and other categories, not only tell stories that illuminate the ruling system, lifestyle, and beliefs of the Chinese ancestors, but at the same time reflect the universality of human experiences that connects cultures. The intertextuality between the exhibition narrative and curatorial practices bridges past and present, embodying the Museum's enduring devotion to enhancing cross-cultural exchanges between civilizations via international collaborations. Museums are important hubs for the preservation and inheritance of civilization, as well as vital platforms for cultural exchange and mutual learning. Expected to travel further, this touring exhibition and more projects upcoming from the *CHINA 100* series of the Shanghai Museum will keep delivering the diverse essence of Chinese art and culture to a broader audience.

引　言

　　罗马帝国时代，欧亚大陆的东端也有一个伟大的王朝——汉（前206年—220年）。汉朝是继秦朝之后的大一统王朝，分西汉、东汉两个时期，历27帝，享国406年。汉朝政治、经济和军事等成就不凡，文学、乐舞、雕塑、书画等硕果斐然，农业、医学、造船、造纸等进步卓著，为后世科技发展和经济艺术繁荣奠定了坚实基础，是中国历史上的黄金时代，也是当时世界上最先进的文明之一，更成为以延续不绝为显著特征的中国历史的重要一环。

　　大量出土及传世文物是追溯这段中华文明华彩的重要依托。"中国汉代文物精品"展以珍贵的玉器、青铜器、陶器、漆器等文物，重现了两汉天下安平、睦邻友邦的大国智慧，百姓殷富、安居乐享的生活气象，以及厌胜辟邪、心系彼岸的精神世界。通过展示两汉王朝掠影，让国际观众更多地了解中国文化之美，感受中华文明的泱泱文脉。

Introduction

At the time of the Roman Empire, another great power thrived at the eastern edge of the Eurasian continent – the Han dynasty (206 BCE – 220 CE), the second great imperial dynasty succeeding the Qin. Separated into two periods – the Western Han (206 BCE – 8 CE) and the Eastern Han (25–220) (interrupted by the Xin period), the dynasty witnessed the reigns of 29 emperors over its 405 years of existence. The Han dynasty notably propelled the imperial's political, economic, and military development. Arts of literature, music, dance, sculpture, calligraphy, and painting made headway. Remarkable achievements unfolded in agriculture, medicine, shipbuilding, and papermaking. These strides built strong groundwork for later eras in technological, economic, and artistic progress, marking the dynasty a golden age in the history of China. As one of the most significant civilizations in the world at that time, the Han dynasty's profound legacies survived and substantially contributed to the continuity of China's history.

The numerous excavated and inherited cultural relics from the Han dynasty are crucial for tracing this cadenza of Chinese civilization. The *Treasures of Han Period China* exhibition displays precious artifacts of jade, bronze, pottery, lacquer, and others, unveiling how the great power governed, how people lived and entertained, and what they believed in and dreamed of. By providing glimpses into the dynasty's essence, the exhibition invites the international audience to the Splerdid world of Chinese culture and connect with the resonant flow of Chinese civilization through the ages.

敦睦的智慧

　　汉承秦制，皇帝之下设三公九卿，进一步推进了向帝制社会的演变。对内，汉朝统治者于建汉之初实行"郡国并行制"，又于其后制衡有方、进退有度地经营数十年，最终建设完善中央集权的官僚制度，成为中国整个帝制时期的楷模。对外，秉持大一统思想的汉王朝加强了对边疆地区的管辖，重视与西域及其他周边国家的通使往来，在外交、经济和军事等领域多有建树，极大提升了中国在古代亚洲的地位。

Wisdom of Ruling

Continuing the Qin system of the Three Councillors of State and Nine Ministers, the Han dynasty further advanced the government towards monarchy. Domestically, the first rulers implemented the "Parallel System of Counties and Feudal Kingdoms", based on which a centralized bureaucratic system matured over decades into an exemplar for later dynasties of imperial China. Externally, Han consolidated its control over border regions with a focus on diplomatic relations and exchanges with the Western Regions and neighboring countries. The Han dynasty saw remarkable accomplishments in diplomacy, economy, and military affairs, significantly enhancing China's status in ancient Asia.

帝陵的建造是一个极为耗费人力和财力的过程。《晋书》载："汉天子即位一年而为陵，天下贡赋三分之，一供宗庙，一供宾客，一充山陵。"陵园的修建与维护有相应的官署与职官来保障。陵园长官称令，可见陵邑规模在万户之上。佐官称丞，尉掌军事。上海博物馆所藏印章中有汉高祖长陵、汉武帝茂陵、汉昭帝平陵、汉元帝渭陵、汉平帝康陵诸陵的陵园名、令、丞、尉用印。

The construction of imperial mausoleums was extremely labor- and resource-intensive. According to the *Book of Jin*, when a Han emperor ascended to the throne, they would start building their mausoleum within the first year, and the tax revenue from the entire country was divided into three parts: one for ancestral temples, one for serving guests, and one for building imperial mausoleums. The construction and maintenance of these mausoleums were supervised by particular officials. The chief official 令 (*ling*) oversaw the mausoleum with the county formed around it, the scale of which might involve tens of thousands of households. Other officials include 丞 (*cheng*) as the assistant to the *ling*, and 尉 (*wei*) as the military officer. The Shanghai Museum houses a collection of seals with names or the aforementioned official titles of mausoleums of Emperor Gaozu, Emperor Wu, Emperor Zhao, Emperor Yuan, and Emperor Kang of Han.

西汉（前 206 年—8 年）

铜

纵 3.20 厘米，横 2.50 厘米，高 1.70 厘米

上海博物馆

Western Han (206 BCE – 8 CE)

Bronze

L. 3.20 cm, W. 2.50 cm, H. 1.70 cm

Shanghai Museum

1 "平陵" 铜印
Seal with Inscription "Ping Ling"

平陵是汉昭帝刘弗陵的帝陵。刘弗陵为汉武帝刘彻的小儿子。在古代，铸造并颁发印章作为身份标识有着一套严格的制度。而这方印章的独特之处在于印面文字为易于辨识的隶书；印章本身不用于抑盖，而是在需要证明身份时出示印章表明身份所属。

Pingling is the imperial mausoleum of Emperor Zhao of Han, Liu Fuling (94–84 BCE), the youngest son of Emperor Wu of Han, Liu Che (156–87 BCE). In ancient China, the casting and issuance of seals as a means of personal identification adhered to a strict system. The distinctive feature of this seal is that the characters on the seal's surface are in easily recognizable clerical script. This seal was not used for stamping but rather served as proof of identity when required.

2 | "康陵园令"铜印
Seal with Inscription "Kang Ling Yuan Ling"

"康陵园令"是掌管汉平帝帝陵——康陵陵园主官所用的官印。陵园令，职官名，汉置，俸六百石。先帝陵，每陵园置令一人，掌守陵园，按行扫除。有丞，为令之副。

This seal is the official seal used by the chief in charge of Kangling, the imperial mausoleum of Emperor Ping of Han (9 BCE – 6 CE). The title of *lingyuan ling* (chief of the imperial mausoleum) was established during the Han dynasty, with an annual salary rank of 600-*dan* (bushels of grain), equivalent to that of a county magistrate. For each imperial mausoleum, a *ling* was designated to guard the mausoleum and oversee its maintenance. Additionally, a *cheng* served as the deputy to the *ling*.

西汉（前 206 年—8 年）
铜
纵 2.40 厘米，横 2.40 厘米，高 2.15 厘米
上海博物馆

Western Han (206 BCE – 8 CE)

Bronze

L. 2.40 cm, W. 2.40 cm, H. 2.150 cm

Shanghai Museum

3

"渭陵园令"铜印
Seal with Inscription "Wei Ling Yuan Ling"

这是汉元帝渭陵陵园主官所用官印。渭陵园令虽掌帝陵，身份特殊，但官位品阶不高，故所用官印仅有桥钮。

This is the official seal used by the chief in charge of Weiling, the imperial mausoleum of Emperor Yuan of Han (74 BCE – 33 CE). Although the *ling* held a special position overseeing the imperial mausoleum, their rank was not particularly high, which is why the seal they used simply has an arch-shaped knob.

西汉（前 206 年—8 年）

铜

纵 2.43 厘米，横 2.43 厘米，高 2.10 厘米

上海博物馆

Western Han (206 BCE – 8 CE)

Bronze

L. 2.43 cm, W. 2.43 cm, H. 2.10 cm

Shanghai Museum

4

"长陵丞印"封泥
Seal Impression of "Chang Ling Cheng Yin"

"丞"是古代各官署长官辅佐官的统称，自中央至郡县均有丞，为副职。

长陵是汉高祖的陵寝。"长陵丞"作为辅佐长陵主官的官员，协助管理整个陵园的运行。这枚"长陵丞印"封泥就是长陵丞用他的官印行使职权时留下的遗物。

Cheng is the general term for officials who assisted the chiefs in government administrations in ancient China, from the central government to the county level, serving as deputy positions.

Changling is the mausoleum of Emperor Gaozu of Han (256–195 BCE). The *Changling cheng* assisted the chief official of Changling in managing the mausoleum's operations. This clay impression witnessed how *Changling cheng* fulfilled his duties using his seal.

西汉（前 206 年—8 年）

泥

纵 2.85 厘米，横 2.58 厘米，高 0.93 厘米

上海博物馆

Western Han (206 BCE – 8 CE)

Clay

L. 2.85 cm, W. 2.58 cm, H. 0.93 cm

Shanghai Museum

5 "茂陵尉印" 石印
Seal with Inscription "Mao Ling Wei Yin"

茂陵是汉武帝的陵寝。"尉"为军尉，因职能不同，细分多种，如太尉掌兵事、廷尉掌刑狱、县尉掌察奸捕盗；又有都尉、卫尉、校尉、骑尉，皆武职，还有中尉等，都简称尉。

茂陵尉，掌管茂陵兵戎以防盗贼。"茂陵尉印"为茂陵尉长官使用的官印。此印石质，印面文字凿刻而成，可能是临时所用。印面文字风格端庄，被中国篆刻爱好者奉为西汉印文的经典之作。

Maoling is the mausoleum of Emperor Wu of Han (156–87 BCE). The title *wei* refers to military officials, and they are further categorized into various positions based on their duties. For example, the *Taiwei* (Grand Commandant) was in charge of military affairs, while the *Tingwei* (Commandant of Justice) oversaw judicial matters. The *Xianwei* (County Commandant) was responsible for investigating and apprehending criminals and thieves. There were also titles like *Duwei* (Commandant of the Capital), *Weiwei* (Commandant of the Guards), *Xiaowei* (Colonel), *Qiwei* (Cavalry Commandant), *Zhongwei* (Commandant-in-Chief), and others, all related to military roles. Collectively, they are known as *wei*.

The *Maoling wei* oversaw the military and security matters at Maoling. This official seal of the title is made of stone, with the characters carved, possibly for temporary use. The characters exhibit an elegant style and are esteemed by Chinese seal engraving enthusiasts as a classic representation of the Western Han dynasty seal script.

西汉（前 206 年—8 年）

石

纵 2.73 厘米，横 2.82 厘米，高 2.27 厘米

上海博物馆

Western Han (206 BCE – 8 CE)

Stone

L. 2.73 cm, W. 2.82 cm, H. 2.27 cm

Shanghai Museum

6 | # 永始二年鼎

Ding (food vessel) with Inscription "The Second Year of Yongshi Reign"

子口内敛，原应有母口盖，颈部设一对直折的附耳，腹部圆鼓，除中腹有一周粗弦纹外光素无纹饰，圜底近平，下置三蹄足，口沿下有铭文："乘舆十涷铜鼎，容一斗，并重十斤四两，永始二年考工工林造，护臣博、守佐军衮、啬夫臣康、掾臣册主，守右丞臣□、守令臣立省。第六十二。"

商周时期鼎是国之重器，属于礼器，发展到汉代，礼器的功能降低，功用发生了很大变化。汉代青铜器已揭去神秘庄重的面纱，礼器比重大减，生活用器的种类和数量增多，汉代青铜器铭文内容也与三代不同，主要是记器主、器名、重量以及容量，有的还有纪年、监造工名、数量序号以及铸造地、铸造机构等。

The vessel's mouth is inwardly curved, originally meant to have a lid. It features a pair of straight-folded lug handles on the neck and a round, bulging belly. The sole decorative element is a coarse cord pattern encircling the belly. The bottom is nearly flat, and it rests on three hoof-shaped feet. The mouth rim bears an inscription that indicates the vessel's weight and its production in 15 BCE, the second year of the Yongshi reign.

During the Shang and Zhou periods, *ding* was an essential type of ritual vessel. However, by the Han dynasty, their ritual significance had waned, and their functions underwent profound changes. Bronzes from the Han dynasty shed their aura of mystery and solemnity, and the variety and quantity of everyday items increased. Inscriptions on Han dynasty bronzes, unlike those of earlier dynasties, primarily provide details about the vessel's owner, its name, weight, and capacity. Some inscriptions also note the year of production, the names of craftsmen, serial numbers, as well as the location and organization of production.

西汉（前 206 年—8 年）

铜

高 15.20 厘米，口径 16.50 厘米，腹径 19.80 厘米，腹深 11.30 厘米

上海博物馆

Western Han (206 BCE – 8 CE)

Bronze

H. 15.20 cm, mouth dia. 16.50 cm,
belly dia. 19.80 cm, belly depth 11.30 cm

Shanghai Museum

上海博物馆『百物看中国』文物艺术出境大展系列

CHINA 100: Outbound Exhibition Series of Arts and Cultures

7 | # 力士三足簋
Gui (food vessel) with Three Figure-shaped Feet

口微侈，折沿尖圆唇，上腹较直，饰四周凸弦纹，第三周凸弦纹较之其他更为凸出；中腹两侧设一对环耳，下腹斜收，腹下接一短圈足；三足为力士造型，力士面部神态清晰，双手扶在胯部，身体微屈，用以支撑鼎腹。

青铜簋作为食器，是青铜器中的一个重要器类，各个时期、各个阶段青铜簋的种类、特征及发展变化规律明显，商代初期的簋是无耳圈足簋，晚商有耳圈足簋流行，发展至西周，出现了柱足簋和方座簋，进入春秋之后，盨取代了簋，成为礼器组合中的食器。此件力士三足簋属于柱足簋的形制。

The vessel has a slightly flared mouth with a protruding sharp rim. Its upper belly is straight and adorned with convex cord patterns, of which the third set protrudes more than the others. The middle has a pair of loop handles attached to its sides. The lower part tapers slightly, leading to a short, circular base. The three feet are in the shape of figures, with clearly visible facial expressions. Their hands are resting on their hips, their bodies slightly bent, holding up the vessel.

Gui as a type of food vessel is a notable category of bronzes. Throughout history, bronze *gui* underwent distinct stages of evolution in types, features, and patterns. In the early Shang dynasty, *gui* had no loop handles or ring foot, while the ones with handles and ring foot became popular during the late Shang dynasty. The Western Zhou saw the emergence of pillar-footed *gui* vessels and those with a square base. Subsequently, during the Spring and Autumn period, *gui* were gradually replaced by *xu* vessels in the ritual bronze ensemble. This piece with three figure-shaped feet belongs to the category of pillar-footed *gui*.

东汉（25 年—220 年）
铜
高 13.50 厘米，口径 23.80 厘米
上海博物馆

Eastern Han (25–220)

Bronze

H. 13.50 cm, mouth dia. 23.80 cm

Shanghai Museum

8 | ## 虎头玉枕饰
Tiger-head-shaped Headrest Ornament

　　此器为楚王玉枕两端的饰件之一。用玉质上乘的青白玉制成，晶莹温润。兽首采用高浮雕和透雕技法雕琢，阔鼻，大口，长眉，双目圆睁，眼球中央浅雕出圆形代表瞳孔。卷曲的双耳从两耳后绕出，额部有高浮雕的冠状饰。构图复杂而严谨，线条流畅而生动，既威严又无恐怖感。楚王玉枕上的玉饰件均由玉质极好的和田玉制成。该玉枕虽尚未修复，但可看出其制作工艺和玉质明显优于同出的"食官监"玉枕和楚王宠妃的玉枕，体现了汉代丧葬用玉的等级差别。

This ornament is one of the embellishments adorning the eifther and of the Chu King's jade headrest. It is crafted from high-quality greenish-white jade, possessing a clear and lustrous appearance. The animal head is meticulously carved in high and openwork relief, featuring a broad nose, a large mouth, long eyebrows, and wide-open eyes with circular pupils. Curled ears extend from behind both sides of the head, and a high-relief coronal decoration adorns the forehead. The composition is intricate yet precise, with smooth lines conveying dignity without invoking fear. The jade adornments on the Chu King's headrest are all made from the finest Hotan jade. While the jade headrest remains unrestored, it is evident that the craftsmanship and jade quality for kings' burial objects surpass those of the contemporary headrests belonging to the *Shiguan jian* (Food Supervisor) and Chu King's concubine unearthed from the same site. This distinction reflects the varying levels of burial jade during the Han dynasty.

西汉（前 206 年—8 年）

玉

长 11.50 厘米，宽 5.80 厘米，高 2.10 厘米

1995 年出土于徐州狮子山楚王墓

徐州博物馆

Western Han (206 BCE – 8 CE)

Jade

L. 11.50 cm, W. 5.80 cm, H. 2.10 cm

Excavated from the Tomb of Chu Kings at Shizishan,

Xuzhou, in 1995

Xuzhou Museum

9 | **玉豹**
Leopard

玉豹以青灰色大理岩雕成，侧卧于台座之上。豹颈脖佩戴镶贝项圈，项圈有系绳环钮。豹目圆睁，肥体健硕，多温驯而少狂野。采用圆雕技法，简洁凝练，概括而传神。汉代帝王有驯养猛兽、圈豹槛虎的风气，各种材质的豹是汉代贵族陵墓中常见的随葬品，也从侧面反映出西汉王侯贵族盛行狩猎。

镇用于压席四角，避免坐、起时折卷席角。镇有大小之别，坐坪压席常用四枚小镇，卧席则用二件大镇。这件玉豹应为楚王当时镇卧席所用，随葬在墓内还应含有驱魅避邪的寓意。

The leopard is carved from bluish-grey marble and lies on its side atop a pedestal. The leopard's neck is in a cowry-inlaid collar fastened with a cord loop. It has round, alert eyes and a robust body, displaying more docility than wildness. Carved in the round, the sculpture is concise and lifelike. During the Han dynasty, there was a practice among emperors of taming fierce beasts, like leopards and tigers, and keeping them as pets. Leopard sculptures made of various materials were commonly found as burial items in the tombs of nobles, reflecting the prevalence of hunting among the aristocracy.

This jade leopard once served as a weight for pressing down the corners of mats, preventing them from curling when people sat or rose. The sizes of these weights vary: four small weights were often used to anchor sitting mats and two large ones for sleeping mats. This leopard is believed to have been used by the Chu King to keep his sleeping mat in place. Burying it in the King's tomb possibly has the symbolism of warding off evil spirits.

西汉（前 206 年—8 年）

玉

长 23.50 厘米，宽 13.00 厘米，高 14.50 厘米

1995 年出土于徐州狮子山楚王墓

徐州博物馆

Western Han (206 BCE – 8 CE)

Jade

L. 23.50 cm, W. 13.00 cm, H. 14.50 cm

Excavated from the Tomb of Chu Kings at Shizishan, Xuzhou, in 1995

Xuzhou Museum

10 | 玉环

Huan (ring)

西汉（前 206 年—8 年）

玉

直径 12.00 厘米，好径 8.20 厘米

1995 年出土于徐州狮子山楚王墓

徐州博物馆

Western Han (206 BCE – 8 CE)

Jade

Dia. 12.00 cm, inner dia. 8.20 cm

Excavated from the Tomb of Chu Kings at Shizishan,

Xuzhou, in 1995

Xuzhou Museum

由新疆和田白玉雕琢而成。两面纹饰相似，雕饰凸起的三周雷纹，构图饱满，简洁有序。

This ring is crafted from white Hotan jade from Xinjiang. It features three layers of thunder patterns intricately carved on both sides, which are well-composed, exuding a sense of simplicity and orderliness.

11 | 玉高足杯
Cup

西汉（前 206 年—8 年）
玉
高 10.90 厘米，直径 4.50 厘米，
内径 3.80 厘米，底径 3.70 厘米
1995 年出土于徐州狮子山楚王墓
徐州博物馆

Western Han (206 BCE – 8 CE)
Jade
H. 10.90 cm, dia. 4.50 cm,
inner dia. 3.80 cm, base dia. 3.70 cm
Excavated from the Tomb of Chu Kings at Shizishan,
Xuzhou, in 1995
Xuzhou Museum

青玉。杯身细而深，略呈上粗下细的圆筒状，足为喇叭形圈足，相对较矮。杯以整玉雕琢而成，杯身素面光洁。玉杯为汉代帝王和贵族珍爱的玉酒具。

The cup has a slender and deep body in a cylindrical shape that tapers down. It stands on a trumpet-shaped ring foot that is relatively short. The cup is meticulously carved from a single piece of green jade, with a smooth and polished surface. Jade cups like this were cherished by emperors and nobles during the Han dynasty as precious drinking vessels.

12 | 玉龙

Dragon

西汉（前 206 年—8 年）

玉

高 13.80 厘米，宽 9.70 厘米，厚 0.48 厘米

1995 年出土于徐州狮子山楚王墓

徐州博物馆

Western Han (206 BCE – 8 CE)

Jade

H. 13.80 cm, W. 9.70 cm, thickness 0.48 cm

Excavated from the Tomb of Chu Kings at Shizishan,

Xuzhou, in 1995

Xuzhou Museum

该龙形佩呈黄色，局部有沁斑。造型为单体龙，腾卷呈 S 形。张须露齿，双目圆睁，鬣毛向两边卷曲，前肢曲折，有钩爪，龙尾上卷并平削，通体饰谷纹。玉龙眼睛下方有一钻孔，为佩戴时的系穿用孔。

This dragon-shaped pendant is yellow in color, bearing localized inclusions. The dragon coils in an S-shape, baring its teeth, with its eyes wide and round and the whiskers curling outwards. The bent front limbs feature claws, and the tail curls upwards and flattens at the end. The entire piece is adorned with grain patterns. There is a drilled hole below the dragon's eyes, which serves as a fastening hole for wearing the pendant.

13 | 玉佩

Pendant

西汉（前 206 年—8 年）

玉

宽 18.80 厘米，高 9.10 厘米

1995 年出土于徐州狮子山楚王墓

徐州博物馆

Western Han (206 BCE – 8 CE)

Jade

W. 18.80 cm, H. 9.10 cm

Excavated from the Tomb of Chu Kings at Shizishan,

Xuzhou, in 1995

Xuzhou Museum

璜体规格较大，满饰谷纹。上弧处两端出廓各透雕一只勾喙回首的凤鸟；下弧内出廓透雕二只颈背相对的凤鸟，鸟尾延至下缘处，并卷尾形成圆孔，凤鸟身下为变形的卷云纹。

This *huang*–pendant is quite big in size and has its surface adorned with intricate grain patterns. Positioned on the upper arc are two phoenixes, each with a hooked beak and turned head. Below the lower arc, another two phoenixes, facing opposite directions, extend their tails to the lower edges that curl to form circular holes. Stylized cloud patterns swirl beneath the birds.

14 双联玉管
Paired Tubes

　　该玉管为两根同样的细长圆管并联而成，两端连接处各以浅浮雕技法雕出兽面纹。兽面双目圆睁，两条长眉毛弯曲上卷，胡须在鼻端对称分布，须尖下弯，鼻子上端延伸出一冠状饰，显得十分威严。玉管中空，两端都饰有勾连云纹，中空磨光，素面。双联玉管由一整块新疆和田青白玉透雕出两管，两端连接部位留出，设计巧妙，琢磨精细，非常少见。一端稍有残缺。

This pair of jade tubes consists of two identical, slender cylindrical tubes joined together, with low–relief carvings of animal masks at the connection points on both ends. The animal masks have round, wide-open eyes, long eyebrows that curl upwards, symmetrical whiskers extending downward from the nose, and a coronal ornament on the upper end of the nose, giving a dignified appearance. The tubes are hollow, adorned with intertwined cloud patterns on both ends, meticulously polished on the inside, and have a smooth surface. This pair of joined tubes is carved from a single piece of greenish-white Hotan jade from Xinjiang, with the connections smartly designed, reflecting exceptional craftsmanship and rarity. One end shows slight damage.

西汉（前 206 年—8 年）

玉

长 26.20 厘米，宽 2.90 厘米

1995 年出土于徐州狮子山楚王墓

徐州博物馆

Western Han (206 BCE – 8 CE)

Jade

L. 26.20 cm, W. 2.90 cm

Excavated from the Tomb of Chu Kings at Shizishan, Xuzhou, in 1995

Xuzhou Museum

上海博物馆「百物看中国」文物艺术出境大展系列

CHINA 100: Outbound Exhibition Series of Arts and Cultures

15 | **卧虎盖三足石砚**
Tripod Inkstone and Lid with a Couchant Tiger

　　青石，分为砚盖与砚体两部分，以子母口相合。盖上雕卧虎，虎作回首状，阴刻圆眼，双耳竖起，鼻前伸，虎口微启；虎身盘绕，上刻条状毛纹；前腿卧伏，一后腿奋力后伸。盖内琢出凹窝，直径2厘米，深1厘米，凹窝内较粗糙，有琢磨痕迹，原应有研石（已失）。砚体中间起一层圆形砚面，砚面高0.2厘米、直径5厘米，砚面平坦，打磨光滑，上留有墨迹。砚底稍带弧形，有三个上大下小的截面呈扇形的圆柱状足，与足相对的砚体上有三个圆堆状突起。

　　东汉时期在圆饼形砚的基础上，发展出三足砚，一方面是对砚的美化，另一方面具有提高砚高度的实际功能。而高浮雕动物盖的出现，除了审美要求之外，既可以延缓墨的干润速度，也能把研石巧妙地纳入盖中。

This limestone inkstone consists of the flanged lid and the body. The lid is carved with a couchant tiger turning its head. It features engraved round eyes, upright ears, a protruding nose, and a slightly open mouth. The tiger's body coils around, with incised stripes representing fur. Its front legs stretch out while one hind leg extends backward. The lid has a recess on the inside, 2 centimeters in diameter and 1 centimeter deep, which has a rough texture with carving marks, suggesting that it once held a grinding stone that is now lost. In the center of the inkstone's body is a circular pool with a height of 0.2 centimeters and a diameter of 5 centimeters. The pool's surface is flat, finely polished, and shows traces of ink. The base is slightly curved and has three cylindrical feet. Three round protrusions on the inkstone body match the feet.

During the Eastern Han dynasty, tripod inkstones were developed from round disk-shaped inkstones, which served both aesthetic and practical purposes, elevating the inkstone's height. The introduction of lids with high-relief animals not only embellishes but also helps to slow down the drying of ink while ingeniously holding the grinding stone within the lid.

东汉（25年—220年）

石

最大径 6.20 厘米，口径 5.80 厘米，连盖高 4.50 厘米

上海博物馆

Eastern Han (25–220)

Stone

Max dia. 6.20 cm, mouth dia. 5.80 cm, H. (with lid) 4.50 cm

Shanghai Museum

16 胡人面具
Figure Mask

东汉（25 年—220 年）

陶

长 12.00 厘米，宽 7.00 厘米，厚 4.00 厘米

2006 年出土于成都金堂李家梁子

成都文物考古研究院

Eastern Han (25–220)

Earthenware

L. 12.00 cm, W. 7.00 cm, thickness 4.00 cm

Excavated from Lijialiangzi, Jintang County,

Chengdu, in 2006

Chengdu Institute of Archaeology

出土于成都金堂李家梁子东汉时期墓葬。泥质灰陶。为胡人面部形象，模制，外凸内凹。胡人戴尖帽，深目，高鼻，颧骨凸出，下巴较尖，络腮胡，面带笑容。两耳后部有一对小孔，应是穿绳所用。该面具可能是汉代用来举行宗教仪式的用具。

This mask was excavated from an Eastern Han dynasty tomb in Lijialiangzi, Jintang County of Chengdu. Molded in grey earthenware, it exhibits the face of a Hu (a term historically used for people from the northern regions). The figure wears a pointed hat, has deep-set eyes, a prominent nose, high cheekbones, a pointed chin, and a beard along the jawline, all while bearing a smiling expression. Behind the ears are a pair of small holes, likely used for threading. The mask was possibly used in religious ceremonies during the Han dynasty.

上海博物馆『百物看中国』文物艺术出境大展系列

CHINA 100: Outbound Exhibition Series of Arts and Cultures

17 兽面云纹玉璧

Bi (disc) with Animal Mask and Cloud Pattern

青白玉，局部有黄褐色沁。玉璧两面纹饰相同，均以绳纹分隔内外两圈，内圈饰谷纹，外圈饰四组等距的兽面纹。兽面一首双身，躯体向两侧卷曲。

《周礼》载："苍璧礼天。"玉璧在古代中国多被用于装饰、馈赠、敛葬等场合，是财富和地位的象征。玉璧流行时间长，自新石器时期至清代均可见使用，此类兽面纹玉璧主要盛行于战国晚期至西汉。

This *bi* is made of greenish-white jade, with yellowish-brown alterations. It displays identical patterns on both sides, divided into two concentric circles by a cord pattern. The inner circle is decorated with grain patterns, while the outer features four evenly spaced animal masks. Each mask leads to double bodies that curl outwards.

According to the *Rites of Zhou*, the *bi* was used in ceremonies for heaven. In ancient China, jade *bi* had various uses, including decoration, gifting, and funerary purposes, symbolizing wealth and status. The popularity of jade *bi* spanned long, from the Neolithic era to the Qing dynasty. Jade *bi* with animal masks like this one were particularly prevalent during the late Warring States period through the Western Han dynasty.

汉（前 206 年—220 年）

玉

径 23.10 厘米，内径 4.70 厘米

上海博物馆

Han (206 BCE – 220 CE)

Jade

Outer dia. 23.10 cm, inner dia. 4.70 cm

Shanghai Museum

上海博物馆『百物看中国』文物艺术出境大展系列

CHINA 100: Outbound Exhibition Series of Arts and Cultures

18 | 青铜钱树

Branches of a Money Tree

钱树，用铜铸造而成的树形制件，大多发现于墓葬中，随葬使用。主要结构有基座、树身主干和周围分叉而出的枝叶，基座陶或石制，树身多用铜铸。方孔圆钱被用来象征财富，装饰在钱树枝叶之间，由于这些铜钱装饰，因此称作"钱树"。在长江中游区域的汉晋时代文化中，钱树主要用来表达一定的民俗信仰，呈现出当时人们想象中的神仙世界。图案中除了方孔圆钱，还常有仙山、西王母、羽人、神鸟、佛像、辟邪、熊龙虎等各种形象，构图常常围绕西王母形象展开，说明钱树既有"西王母文化"崇拜，也有对钱币象征财富的追求意识。

A "money tree" is a tree-shaped bronze artefact, often found in burials. It consists of several key components: a base, a trunk, from which branches and leaves grow. The base is made of pottery or stone; the tree trunk, commonly cast in bronze. Round coins with square holes embellish the branches and leaves as a symbol of wealth, giving the artefact the name of a "money tree". In the culture of the Han and Jin dynasties in the middle reaches of the Yangtze River, the money tree represents folk beliefs in an imagined world of immortals and deities. The designs feature not only coins but also various other motifs, such as sacred mountains, the Queen Mother of the West, winged immortals, divine birds, Buddha statues, mythical creatures, and beasts like bears, dragons, and tigers. The compositions often revolve around the imagery of the Queen Mother of the West, indicating that the money tree was related with the worship of the goddess in addition to the pursuit of wealth symbolized by the coins.

东汉（25 年—220 年）

铜

长 20.00—30.00 厘米，宽 10.00—15.00 厘米

上海博物馆

Eastern Han (25–220)

Bronze

L. 20.00–30.00 cm, W. 10.00–15.00 cm

Shanghai Museum

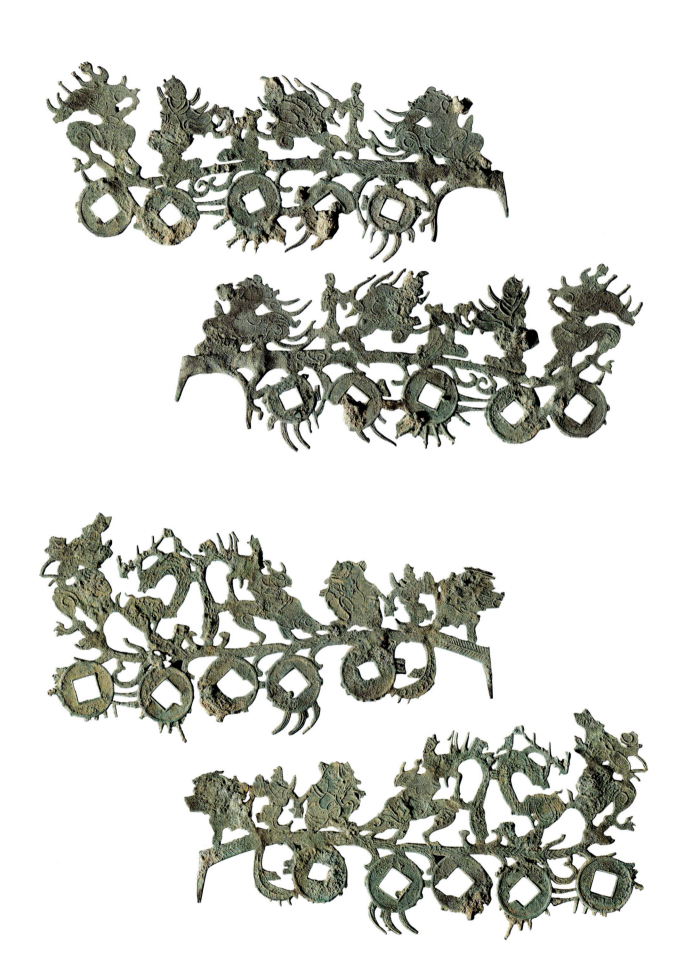

19 | 五铢钱
Wu Zhu Coins

汉王朝的制式货币。至公元前 113 年，中国的货币铸造权开始统一于国家中央，统一的型式，逐渐趋同的重量，深远影响了中国古代钱币文化。形式方面，圆形方孔，边缘处都设计了廓边，汉字"五铢"左右对称布局。重量上，钱币逐步固定在每枚 3.5—4.0 克左右。五铢钱的铸造和发行说明了国家经济力量强大。在不少墓葬中，墓主会随葬用于死后"生活"中的硬通货——五铢钱，许多五铢铜钱被放置于墓葬的棺椁内外。

Wu Zhu is the standardized currency of the Han dynasty. By the year 113 BCE, the government began to centralize the authority to mint coins in China, leading to their standardized forms and weights, which profoundly impacted ancient Chinese numismatic culture. In terms of design, these coins are typically circular with square holes and feature raised rims along the edges. The characters 五铢 (*wu zhu*, "five zhu") were symmetrically arranged on both sides. In terms of weight, the coins eventually became standardized to around 4 grams each. The production and circulation of Wu Zhu coins reflected the state's robust economy. In many tombs, Wu Zhu coins accompany the deceased as the "hard currency" for their afterlife needs. Numerous Wu Zhu coins have been found both inside and outside burial coffins.

东汉（25 年—220 年）

铜

径 2.00—2.50 厘米

上海博物馆

Eastern Han (25–220)

Bronze

Dia. 2.00–2.50 cm

Shanghai Museum

上海博物馆『百物看中国』文物艺术出境大展系列

CHINA 100: Outbound Exhibition Series of Arts and Cultures

玉剑具是中国古代装饰于剑柄及剑鞘上的玉饰件。始于西周，至东周两汉盛行一时。一套完整的玉剑具包括玉剑首、玉剑格、玉璏和玉珌等。其中，玉剑首嵌于剑柄顶端，常见圆饼形；玉剑格饰于剑身与剑柄之间，作护手之用；玉璏镶于剑鞘外部中上端，可穿入革带以佩剑于腰间；玉珌安于剑鞘尾端，造型多样，以梯方束腰形常见。

剑具是古代贵族身份、地位的象征之一。制作剑具的材质除软玉外，还可见琉璃、玛瑙、萤石、绿松石、黄金、青铜、竹木等。材质的珍稀程度与佩戴者的身份等级密切相关。汉代以玉作装饰的剑多出土于诸侯王、列侯墓中。

Jade sword fittings are decorative jade ornaments on the hilt and scabbard of ancient Chinese swords. The practice of adorning swords with jade began during the Western Zhou period and became popular during the Eastern Zhou and Han dynasties. A complete set of jade sword fittings typically includes the pommel attached to the top of the hilt, often in a round shape; the guard between the blade and hilt; the scabbard slide threaded with a leather belt for wearing the sword at the waist; and the chape at the end of the scabbard, commonly in a trapezoid shape.

Sword fittings symbolized the status of nobility in ancient times. Besides jade, they come in colored glaze, agate, fluorite, turquoise, gold, bronze, bamboo, and wood. The rarity of the material reveals the rank and status of the wearer. Swords adorned with jade were frequently unearthed in the tombs of dukes and marquises.

20 | 谷纹玉剑首
Sword Pommel with Grain Pattern

青玉，局部有黑褐色沁。正面内圈圆上琢四组云纹，外圈饰以谷纹，饱满自然，排列规则有序。谷纹始见于春秋时期，流行于战国至秦汉，多以减地隐起技法琢刻。

This piece of green jade, with blackish-brown alterations, features four sets of swirling cloud patterns on the inner circle of the front side. The outer circle is adorned with grain patterns, plump and orderly arranged. Grain patterns first appeared during the Spring and Autumn period and became popular from the Warring States period through the Qin and Han dynasties. They were often carved using a low-relief technique that reduces the depth of the background while highlighting the raised motifs.

汉（前 206 年—220 年）

玉

直径 3.30 厘米，厚 0.50 厘米

上海博物馆

Han (206 BCE – 220 CE)

Jade

Dia. 3.30 cm, thickness 0.50 cm

Shanghai Museum

21 云纹玉剑首
Sword Pommel with Cloud Pattern

白玉，局部有赭红色沁。正面内圈剔地凸起，等距琢有四组云纹，间以丝束纹，中心为菱形纹，外圈光素无纹。背面内圈中心有一圆形凹槽，周边等距钻有三个穿孔，以便嵌入剑柄，外圈以阴刻线琢对称的八个简化的龙首纹，龙首纹两两鼻口相对。玉剑首一般背面光素无纹，偶见背面外圈饰有勾连云纹、龙首纹等纹饰。

This piece of white jade, with reddish-brown alterations, features a raised inner circle on the front side, where four sets of equidistant cloud patterns are meticulously carved, separated by fine twisted spiral patterns. In the center are diamond-shaped patterns, while the outer circle is plain and unadorned. On the reverse, the central part of the inner circle contains a circular depression, surrounded by three evenly spaced slots for securing it to a sword hilt. The outer circle is carved with eight simplified dragon head motifs symmetrically arranged by incised lines. These dragon heads face each other in pairs. Jade sword pommels typically have a plain reverse, but occasionally, the outer circle on the back may feature decorative patterns such as intertwined cloud patterns or dragon head motifs.

汉（前 206 年—220 年）

玉

直径 5.70 厘米，厚 1.50 厘米

上海博物馆

Han (206 BCE – 220 CE)

Jade

Dia. 5.70 cm, thickness 1.50 cm

Shanghai Museum

22 | 螭纹玉剑首
Sword Pommel with *Chi*-dragon (hornless dragon)

青白玉，局部有灰黄色及黑褐色沁。正面浮雕一盘旋的螭纹，螭首刻画精细，大眼阔鼻，须发后曳，前肢健硕有力，螭身卷曲，绞丝长尾。背面光素，内圈中心有一圆形凹槽，周边钻有四个穿孔，以便嵌入剑柄。

螭为龙属，是中国传统吉祥图案之一，也是高贵、权威的象征。螭纹始见于春秋晚期，战国时期形象多变，尚未完全定型，至汉代逐渐成熟。汉代玉剑饰中螭纹常见，且多以高浮雕手法表现，此玉剑首中呈盘旋造型的螭纹较为稀有。

This piece of greenish-white jade, with greyish-yellow and blackish-brown alterations, features a coiled *chi*-dragon (a hornless dragon) in relief on the front side. The dragon's head is finely carved with wide eyes, a broad nose, and trailing hair and whiskers. It has muscular forelimbs, a coiled body, and a long, twisted tail. The back side is plain, with a central circular depression in the inner circle, surrounded by four slots for securing it to a sword hilt.

The *chi*, belonging to the dragon family, is one of the traditional auspicious motifs in China and symbolizes nobility and authority. *Chi*-dragon motifs first appeared in the late Spring and Autumn period, went through different variants during the Warring States, and gradually matured in the Han dynasty. *Chi*-dragon motifs were commonly found in Han dynasty jade sword decorations, often presented in high relief. The coiled *chi*-dragon is rarely found on a jade sowrd pommel.

汉（前 206 年—220 年）

玉

直径 3.85 厘米

上海博物馆

Han (206 BCE – 220 CE)

Jade

Dia. 3.85 cm

Shanghai Museum

23 | 兽面纹玉剑格
Sword Guard with Animal Mask

东汉（25 年—220 年）

玉

长 6.10 厘米，宽 2.30 厘米，高 1.40 厘米

上海博物馆

Eastern Han (25–220)

Jade

L. 6.10 cm, W. 2.30 cm, H. 1.40 cm

Shanghai Museum

青白玉。器身两面均以尖脊为中心，浅浮雕一兽面，粗眉后曳，大眼微凸，楔形宽鼻，嘴角上卷。兽面两侧装饰有云纹，纹饰对称分布。

This piece is made of greenish-white jade. Ridges rise at the cener on both sides, with a symmetrical animal mask in low relief. It features thick eyebrows that extend backward, large protruding eyes, a wide V-shaped nose, and a mouth with upturned corners. The animal mask is flanked by symmetrical cloud patterns.

24 兽面纹玉剑格
Sword Guard with Animal Mask

东汉（25 年—220 年）

玉

长 5.50 厘米，宽 1.70 厘米，高 2.40 厘米

上海博物馆

Eastern Han (25–220)

Bronze

L. 5.50 cm, W. 1.70 cm, H. 2.40 cm

Shanghai Museum

　　白玉，玉质细腻。器身两面均以尖脊为中心，浅浮雕一兽面，绳纹粗眉，大眼宽鼻，阔嘴。兽面两侧各饰三组云纹。此类纹饰于汉代玉剑格上常见，在兽面的细节、云纹的组合上不尽相同。

This piece of white jade exhibits excellent quality. Ridges rise at the cener on both sides, with a symmetrical animal mask in low relief. The mask features thick eyebrows, large eyes, a wide nose, and a broad mouth, flanked by three sets of cloud patterns. Such motifs are commonly seen on Han dynasty jade sword guards and vary in the details of the animal mask and the arrangement of cloud patterns.

上海博物馆『百物看中国』文物艺术出境大展系列

CHINA 100: Outbound Exhibition Series of Arts and Cultures

25 | 云纹玉剑格
Sword Guard with Cloud Pattern

汉（前 206 年—220 年）

玉

长 5.70 厘米，高 1.60 厘米

上海博物馆

Han (206 BCE – 220 CE)

Jade

L. 5.70 cm, H. 1.60 cm

Shanghai Museum

青白玉，受沁较严重，呈灰白色。器身两面均以尖脊为中心，减地浅浮雕多组对称的变形云纹，间饰有双阴刻线，线条刚劲有力。

This piece of greenish-white jade has prominent alterations resulting in a greyish-white hue. Ridges rise at the cener on both sides, with multiple symmetrical sets of modified cloud patterns in low relief. The patterns are alternated with double incised lines in a robust appearance.

26 | 兽面云纹玉璏

Scabbard Slide with Animal Mask and Cloud Pattern

汉（前 206 年—220 年）

玉

长 7.80 厘米，宽 2.40 厘米，高 1.40 厘米

上海博物馆

Han (206 BCE – 220 CE)

Jade

L. 7.80 cm, W. 2.40 cm, H. 1.40 cm

Shanghai Museum

白玉，玉质细腻。玉璏上部呈拱形，两端内卷，下部有一长方形穿孔，是汉代最为常见的玉璏形制之一。器面上端饰一绳纹粗眉、大眼的兽面，兽面中心线两旁饰有左右对称的云纹，辅以双阴刻线装饰。

This piece of white jade exhibits excellent quality. The top of it forms an arch with both ends curling inward, while the lower part has a rectangular slot. It is one of the most common types of jade scabbard slide during the Han dynasty. On the panel is an animal mask with thick eyebrows and large eyes, flanked by symmetrical cloud patterns in double incised lines.

上海博物馆『百物看中国』文物艺术出境大展系列

CHINA 100: Outbound Exhibition Series of Arts and Cultures

27 | 螭云纹玉璏

Scabbard Slide with *Chi*-dragon (hornless dragon) and Cloud Pattern

青白玉，局部有赭红色沁。器表浮雕大小二螭穿云而行，勇武矫健。母螭约占器面三分之二，大眼直鼻，犬耳，四肢有力，尾部绞丝卷曲。小螭与母螭相向而行，面部细节相似，后肢健硕，毛发刻划清晰。子母螭是汉代最为流行的纹样之一。

This piece of greenish-white jade, with reddish-brown alterations, depicts two *chi*-dragons (hornless dragons) roaming through the clouds with a vigorous demeanor. The mother dragon occupies approximately two-thirds of the surface, featuring large eyes, a straight nose, canine ears, powerful limbs, and a coiled tail. The smaller dragon faces its mother, sharing similar facial details, with sturdy hind limbs and finely carved hair. The motif of the *chi*-dragon mother and her cub is one of the most popular from the Han dynasty.

西汉（前 206 年—8 年）

玉

长 10.90 厘米，宽 2.60 厘米，高 2.00 厘米

上海博物馆

Western Han (206 BCE – 8 CE)

Jade

L. 10.90 cm, W. 2.60 cm, H. 2.00 cm

Shanghai Museum

28

螭纹玉璏
Scabbard Slide with *Chi*-dragon (hornless dragon)

汉（前 206 年—220 年）

玉

长 9.70 厘米，宽 2.30 厘米，高 2.30 厘米

上海博物馆

Han (206 BCE – 220 CE)

Jade

L. 9.70 cm, W. 2.30 cm, H. 2.30 cm

Shanghai Museum

青白玉。器表浮雕大小二螭相向而行，母螭大眼直鼻，须发后曳，前肢前屈，后肢一前一后呈弓状张开，矫健有力，螭身中脊阴刻，长尾后摆。小螭蜷曲回首，灵动活泼。

This piece of greenish-white jade features high-relief carvings of two *chi*-dragons facing each other. The mother dragon has large eyes, a straight nose, and trailing whiskers, with its forelimbs bent forward and hind limbs extended in a bow-like posture, exuding agility and strength. Its body has a central ridge in incised lines, and a long tail trailing behind. The smaller *chi*-dragon is coiled, turning its head back, and appears lively and cheerful.

上海博物馆『百物看中国』文物艺术出境大展系列

CHINA 100: Outbound Exhibition Series of Arts and Cultures

29   **兽面云纹玉璏**

Scabbard Slide with Animal Mask and Cloud Pattern

青玉，局部有赭红色沁。整体呈一较短的穿孔长方体，上部略拱，穿孔下边略窄，是汉代常见的玉璏形制之一。器面中脊高凸，两侧浅浮雕一粗眉大眼的兽面纹饰，兽面之上为勾连云纹，纹饰对称分布。

This piece of green jade, with reddish-brown alterations, takes the shape of a short cuboid with a slot. The top subtly arches, while the lower part of the slot slightly tapers, representing one of the common forms of jade scabbard slides from the Han dynasty. The central ridge on the surface is prominently raised, flanked by an animal mask in low relief with thick eyebrows and large eyes. Above the mask are symmetrical interlocking cloud patterns.

汉（前 206 年—220 年）

玉

长 2.80 厘米，宽 2.10 厘米，高 4.90 厘米

上海博物馆

Han (206 BCE – 220 CE)

Jade

L. 2.80 cm, W. 2.10 cm, H. 4.90 cm

Shanghai Museum

30

云纹玉珌
Scabbard Chape with Cloud Pattern

汉（前 206 年—220 年）

玉

长 5.50 厘米，宽 1.80 厘米，高 4.50 厘米

上海博物馆

Han (206 BCE – 220 CE)

Jade

L. 5.50 cm, W. 1.80 cm, H. 4.50 cm

Shanghai Museum

青玉，局部有土黄色沁。整体作梯方造型，两腰略收，顶面钻有三个相连之孔，以供与剑鞘连接。器身两面浅浮雕有对称分布的云纹，间饰有双阴刻线。底部阴刻一组对称的云纹。

This piece of green jade, with earthy yellow alterations, features a trapezoid shape, slightly tapered at the waist. The top surface is pierced with three interconnected holes, intended for attachment to a scabbard. On both sides of the chape are symmetrical cloud patterns in low relief, embellished with double incised lines. The bottom is incised with a set of symmetrical cloud patterns.

上海博物馆『百物看中国』文物艺术出境大展系列

CHINA 100: Outbound Exhibition Series of Arts and Cultures

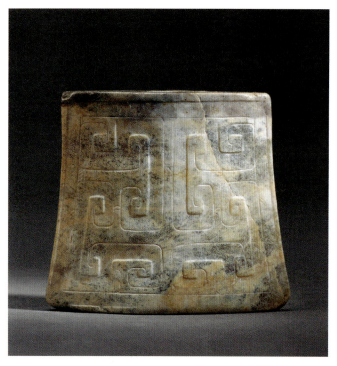
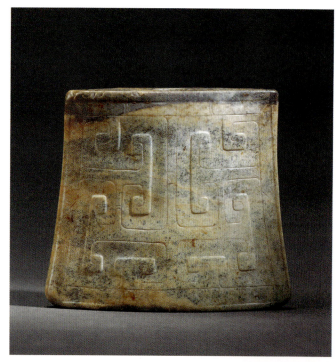

31 | 勾连云纹玉珌

Scabbard Chape with Interlocked Cloud Pattern

汉（前 206 年—220 年）

玉

长 5.00 厘米，宽 4.40 厘米

上海博物馆

Han (206 BCE – 220 CE)

Jade

L. 5.00 cm, W. 4.40 cm

Shanghai Museum

青玉，分布有墨黑色包裹体，局部有灰黄色沁。呈梯方造型，两腰略收，顶部钻有一孔。器身双面浅浮雕对称的勾连云纹，辅以阴刻细纹。底部阴刻一组勾连云纹。

This piece of green jade, with scattered black indusions and greyish-yellow alterations, features a trapezoid shape, slightly tapered at the waist. There is a hole drilled at the top. On both sides of the chape are symmetrical interlocking cloud patterns in low relief, complemented by subtly incised lines. The bottom is incised with a set of interlocking cloud patterns.

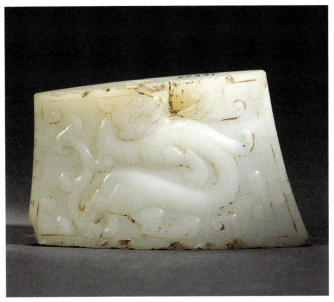

32　龙纹珌
Scabbard Chape with Dragon Pattern

琉璃，乳白色。整体呈斜方梯形，一角残缺，顶部钻有一孔。器身正面浮雕一侧身龙纹，龙大眼阔鼻张嘴，脖颈与龙身弯折，矫健有力，长尾分叉卷曲上摆，整体线条流畅，背面浅浮雕对称分布的勾连云纹。底部阴刻勾连云纹。

Crafted from coloured glaze, this piece exhibits a milky white hue. It takes on an oblique trapezoidal shape, with one corner damaged, and has a hole drilled at the top. On the front of it is a high-relief carving of a side-facing dragon. The dragon features large eyes, a broad nose, an open mouth, and a sinuous neck that gracefully curves with the body, conveying strength and agility. The dragon's long tail is forked and curls upward. The overall design boasts smooth, flowing lines. On the back are symmetrical interlocking cloud patterns in low relief. The bottom is incised with interlocking cloud patterns.

汉（前 206 年—220 年）

琉璃

长 7.50 厘米，宽 4.70 厘米

上海博物馆

Han (206 BCE – 220 CE)

Coloured glaze

L. 7.50 cm, W. 4.70 cm

Shanghai Museum

贰 Part II

生活的艺术

　　在儒家思想的影响和安居乐享的社会氛围下，汉朝手工业水平长足进步，器物制作渐重实用，并在饰纹和造型中融入对世界的观察与日常巧思。物阜民丰，宴飨之风盛行。王侯贵族盛装华饰，觞酒豆食，箫笙伴耳。平民百姓提壶行酤，怡然自得。在浮雕刻绘的汉砖石阙、光彩于纹的漆杯圆盘和大道至简的钩环佩玉之间，大汉王朝的生活万象跃然而现。

Art of Living

The Han dynasty once again unified the country after the Qin dynasty. Under the influence of Confucianism, the stable soriety of the Han dynasty fostered significant progress in the handicraft industry. Artisans turned to prioritize the practicality of utensils, incorporating their perceptions and ingenuity into the patterns and designs. The prosperity of material life allowed a celebratory culture to thrive. Earthenware vessels were widely used in the joyful daily lives of commoners. Meanwhile, nobles adorned their days with elegant costumes and objects. Intricate or modest, the reliefs, lacquers, and jades capture a kaleidoscope of the myriad aspects of life in the Han dynasty.

33 | 双阙画像砖
Brick with Two *Que* (towers)

东汉（25 年—220 年）

陶

长 45.00 厘米，宽 41.00 厘米，厚 6.50 厘米

2001 年出土于成都西窑村汉墓

成都文物考古研究院

Eastern Han (25–220)

Earthenware

L. 45.00 cm, W. 41.00 cm, thickness 6.50 cm

Excavated from the Han-dynasty tombs at Xiyaocun,

Chengdu, in 2001

Chengdu Institute of Archaeology

出土于成都西窑村东汉时期砖室墓中。画面主体由双阙构成，母阙重檐，其外侧各有一子阙，双阙以桥形层楼连接，楼下大门呈开启状态。层楼之上立一展翅凤鸟。

This brick excavated from an Eastern Han brick-chamber tomb in Xiyaocun, Chengdu, features a scene of two *que* (gate towers). The main towers have double eaves, with a subsidiary tower on each side. The two towers are connected by a bridge-like multi-story structure, and the gates beneath it are open. Atop the linking structure stands a bird with outstretched wings.

34 | **龙纹空心砖**
Hollow Brick with Dragon

西汉（前 206 年—8 年）
陶
纵 106.00 厘米，横 84.00 厘米
上海博物馆

Western Han (206 BCE – 8 CE)

Earthenware

L. 106.00 cm, W. 84.00 cm

Shanghai Museum

空心砖呈三角形，正面模印弯曲的一条龙，四周和侧面模印菱格纹作为装饰。这类空心砖多出土于西汉时期的砖室墓，以洛阳出土为多。

This triangular hollow brick features a curved dragon imprinted on the front and diamond-shaped lattice patterns along the four sides and on the lateral surfaces. This type of hollow bricks is commonly excavated from brick-chamber tombs of the Western Han dynasty, with many being found in Luoyang.

35 人物御龙空心砖
Hollow Brick with Figure Riding a Dragon

空心砖呈三角形，正面模印弯曲的一条龙，龙身之上一仙人左手持剑，右手持盾御龙，四周和侧面模印菱格纹作为装饰。仙人御龙题材与战国、两汉流行的神仙思想有关。

This triangular hollow brick features a curved dragon imprinted on the front. Above the dragon stands a deity wielding a sword in the left hand and a shield in the right hand, controlling the dragon. Decorative diamond-shaped lattice patterns are imprinted along the four sides and on the lateral surfaces. The motif of a deity controlling a dragon is associated with the prevalent concept of immortality and deities during the Warring States period and Han dynasty.

西汉（前 206 年—8 年）

陶

纵 107.00 厘米，横 80.00 厘米

上海博物馆

Western Han (206 BCE – 8 CE)

Earthenware

L. 107.00 cm, W. 80.00 cm

Shanghai Museum

36 | 鸭首壶

Hu (pot) with Duck-head-shaped Spout

壶首作鸭头状，头部可见圆突而传神的双目，扁状嘴巴微微张开。长颈弯曲成流畅的 "C" 字形，颈部最高处开圆孔，脖颈中部有一段较薄的圆箍，圆箍中部饰一周粗状凸弦纹。扁圆腹，腹部较鼓，光素无纹，下置外侈高圈足。整体造型十分灵动逼真，兼具实用性和装饰性，体现了汉代工匠高超的技艺和汉代青铜器生活化的趋向。

此类鸭首壶战国时期就已经出现，出土于合阳县灵井村、现藏于渭南市博物馆的战国鸭头铜壶，整体形态与该器颇为相似，唯其鸭头与颈部成垂直状，稍有不同。

The pot spout is shaped like a duck's head, featuring round, expressive eyes and a slightly open, flat beak. The long neck gracefully curves into a C shape, with a round hole at the highest point. In the middle lies a thin circular band adorned with a coarse convex ring. The bulging belly, devoid of decoration, rests on a high ring foot. The overall design is remarkably lifelike and dynamic, showcasing both practicality and decorative artistry. It reflects the exceptional craftsmanship of Han dynasty artisans and the trend of practical everyday use in bronze objects from that time.

Pots with duck-head-shaped spouts were already present during the Warring States period. An example is the one excavated from Lingjingcun, Heyang County, in Weinan of Shaanxi province, now housed in the Weinan Museum. While it shares an overall resemblance with this piece, the duck head and neck are oriented vertically.

汉（前 206 年—220 年）

铜

高 25.10 厘米，口径 2.90 厘米，
腹径 19.60 厘米，底径 10.90 厘米

上海博物馆

Han (206 BCE – 220 CE)

Bronze

H. 25.10 cm, mouth dia. 2.90 cm,
belly dia. 19.60 cm, base dia. 10.90 cm

Shanghai Museum

37 | 彩绘陶茧形壶
Cocoon-shaped *Hu* (pot)

撇口，短颈，茧形腹，高圈足。灰陶胎，胎质细腻。通体纵向划有细密弦纹，并施白色及红色彩绘装饰。

茧形壶是战国秦汉时期流行的一种形状独特的器型，由于其腹部的形状类似蚕茧，因而得名茧形壶。茧形壶自战国中期首先出现在陕西关中地区，随后向周围扩散，最早的茧形壶是圆底，稍后才出现圈足。战国晚期至秦统一时期发展到鼎盛阶段，西汉早期延续，西汉中期消失，前后流行时段约三个世纪。

考古出土的茧形壶以陕西地区最多，此外，在甘肃、山西、河南、山东、江苏、湖北等地也有发现，多为陶制，以墓葬出土为主，少数出土于遗址中的水井、窖藏，也有零星的采集品。

This pot has a flared mouth, a short neck, a cocoon-shaped body, and a high ring foot. Made of gray pottery with a fine texture, it is decorated with intricate, vertical string patterns and painted in white and red colors.

The cocoon-shaped pot is a unique type of vessel popular during the Warring States and Qin-Han periods. It earned its name due to its belly resembling a silkworm cocoon. Such vessels first appeared in the central Shaanxi region during the mid-Warring States period and then spread to surrounding areas. The earliest ones had round bottoms, and ring feet emerged later. During the late Warring States to early Qin, they reached their peak in popularity, continued into the early Western Han period, and disappeared by the middle Western Han period. This distinctive style prevailed over approximately three centuries.

Archaeological findings of cocoon-shaped pots are most abundant in the Shaanxi region. They have also been discovered in Gansu, Shanxi, Henan, Shandong, Jiangsu, Hubei, and other areas. These pots are primarily unearthed from tombs, with a few found in ancient wells and hoards at archaeological sites, as well as several acquired examples.

汉（前 206 年—220 年）

陶

高 45.00 厘米，宽 40.00 厘米，
口径 11.80 厘米，底径 12.20 厘米

上海博物馆

倪汉克先生捐赠

Han (206 BCE – 220 CE)

Painted earthenware

H. 45.00 cm, W. 40.00 cm,
mouth dia. 11.80 cm, base dia. 12.20 cm

Shanghai Museum

Gift of Mr. Henk Nieuwenhuys

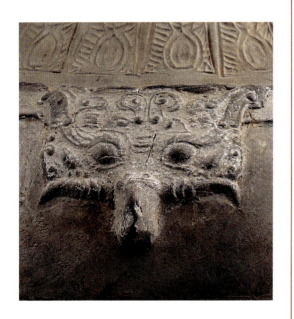

汉（前 206 年—220 年）

陶

高 42.10 厘米，宽 31.50 厘米，

口径 19.30 厘米，底径 19.20 厘米

上海博物馆

倪汉克先生捐赠

Han (206 BCE – 220 CE)

Grey earthenware

H. 42.10 cm, W. 31.50 cm,

mouth dia. 19.30 cm, base dia. 19.20 cm

Shanghai Museum

Gift of Mr. Henk Nieuwenhuys

38 灰陶壶

Hu (pot)

灰陶胎，胎质坚硬。盘口，长束颈，鼓腹，腹下内收，高圈足。颈部装饰蕉叶纹，腹部的主题纹饰分上下两段，均为骑马狩猎纹，中间以凸起的宽弦纹隔开，两侧对贴铺首。整体纹饰的装饰技法为印花装饰，铺首为模印贴塑。

此类造型为仿同时期铜壶的造型，带盖。在汉代，此类器有自铭为壶者，多用以盛酒。《周礼·掌客》郑玄注："壶，酒器也。"马王堆 1 号墓的遣策中也说"鬃画壶二，皆有盖，盛米酒"。但洛阳烧沟汉墓中出土的陶壶盛放粮食，满城汉墓出土的陶壶中有动物骨骼，可见壶也可用于盛放其他食物。

This pot is made of grey pottery, with a hard texture. It has a flat mouth, a long slender neck, a bulging body that tapers inward at the lower part, and a high ring-shaped foot. The neck is adorned with patterns of banana leaves. The main motif on the belly is divided into upper and lower sections, both featuring horseback hunting scenes. These scenes are separated by raised wide string patterns. Animal-shaped appliques are attached to each side of the pot. The overall decorations use the technique of stamping, with the appliques being molded and adhered.

This type of vessel imitates the shape of contemporary bronze pots, often with a lid. During the Han dynasty, some of these vessels were inscribed as *hu* (壶), mainly used for holding wine. According to the *Rites of Zhou*, the *hu* is a wine container. The burial inventory from the Mawangdui Tomb No. 1 also mentions "two painted lacquer *hu* with lids, used for holding rice wine". However, the pottery pots excavated from Han dynasty tombs in Luoyang once stored grains, while animal bones were discovered in the ones found from tombs in Mancheng, indicating that *hu* were also containers for storing other types of food.

39 | 羊灯
Ram-shaped Lamp

整体造型为曲膝跪卧的羊形，背部打开可为灯盘。羊头微微昂起，羊角绕耳内卷，紧贴面颊，眼睛呈扁圆状，鼻孔较圆，胡须直垂到胸前，后置短尾，紧贴臀部。全身錾刻或长或短的线条纹，细密柔和，颇似羊毛。体态壮硕，丰满浑圆，远观古朴稳重，静怡安详；近看温顺可爱，形象逼真；外观设计乖巧，颇为惹人喜爱。

卧羊铜灯主要流行于西汉时期，是一种设计巧妙的灯具，羊身由羊背和腹腔组合而成，二者通过颈后的活轴连接。当使用时，将羊背翻至头顶。当不使用时，将羊背下翻合拢。卧羊铜灯是将实用性、科学性、艺术性及思想性融为一体的智慧之作。

The lamp takes on the shape of a recumbent ram, with its back serving as a lamp tray when opened. The ram's head is slightly raised, its horns curling inward around the ears, snugly against its cheeks. The eyes are oval-shaped, the nostrils rounded. It has a straight beard hanging down to its chest and a short tail clinging to its hindquarters. The entire body is carved with lines of varying lengths, creating a meticulous and soft texture reminiscent of sheep's wool. Its physique is robust and plump, giving an appearance dignified and serene from a distance while lifelike and endearing upon closer inspection.

The sheep-shaped lamp was popular mainly during the Western Han for its ingenious design. The sheep's body consists of its back and abdominal cavity, connected by a pivot joint behind the neck. When in use, the back can be flipped over the head to reveal the lamp tray. It is a masterpiece that combines practicality, scientific ingenuity, artistic aesthetics, and philosophical symbolism.

汉（前 206 年—220 年）

铜

长 12.00 厘米，高 9.30 厘米

上海博物馆

Han (206 BCE – 220 CE)

Bronze

L. 12.00 cm, H. 9.30 cm

Shanghai Museum

40 | 雁足灯
Lamp with Goose-foot-shaped Stand

整体由灯盘、灯柱、雁足灯座三部分组成，灯盘圆凹，内圈中空，灯座雁爪造型有力，前面三爪较长，后面小爪的细节刻画到位，灯柱关节形象逼真，整体透露出一种科学与准确感，展现出皇家之器的庄重与大气。灯盘外底有一周刻铭，从铭文可知此灯制造于西汉竟宁元年（前 33 年），为皇后之宫所有。

青铜雁足灯从战国晚期开始铸造使用，一直到东汉末期，战国时期和西汉时期的雁足灯十分具象。铭文记载了当时的材料所耗、制作与监管官员等信息，是汉代物勒工名制度的见证。

The lamp consists of three parts: the tray, the column, and the goose-foot base. The tray is concave with a hole in the middle. The base features a powerful goose foot. The front three toes are long, and the hind toe is meticulously carved in detail. The "joints" on the lamp column are lifelike and precise in form. The design exudes the dignity and grandeur of a royal artefact. The inscription on the bottom of the lamp tray indicates that this lamp was made in the first year of the Jingning reign during the Western Han (33 BCE) and belonged to the queen's palace.

Bronze lamps with goose-foot designs were crafted and used from the late Warring States period through the late Eastern Han. During the Warring States and Western Han, these lamps were highly realistic in design. The inscription records information such as the materials used and the officials responsible for production and supervision, serving as evidence of the quality management system of artisans putting down their names during the Han dynasty.

西汉（前 206 年—8 年）

铜

高 24.00 厘米，盘径 13.85 厘米

上海博物馆

Western Han (206 BCE – 8 CE)

Bronze

H.24.00 cm, base dia. 13.85 cm

Shanghai Museum

41

绿釉陶熊灯
Lamp with Bear-shaped Stem

红陶胎，通体施铅绿釉，具有较强的装饰效果。由灯盏、灯柱和灯座三部分组成。灯盏为一圆形平盘，灯座呈喇叭形，最引人注目的是一对蹲坐的母子熊灯柱，母熊熊头硕大，口微张，憨态可掬。此种熊灯在甘肃、陕西、河南、宁夏等地均有出土。

灯现在一般认为是从食器中的豆转化来的，《尔雅·释器》中有："木豆谓之豆，竹豆谓之笾，瓦豆谓之登。"郭璞注："即膏灯也。"我国使用灯具的历史十分悠久，油灯作为传统的生活用具，在几千年的历史长河中发展，在各时期形成了不同的特色。

汉代是古代灯具发展的重要时期，此时的灯构思奇巧、式样丰富，为历代灯具所不能及，主要造型有豆形灯、浅盘形灯、多支灯、动物形灯、耳杯形灯、卮形灯、钉灯等，常用陶、铜、铁等材质制成。

This lamp has a red clay body coated in green lead glaze, creating a strong decorative effect. It consists of three parts: the dish, the column, and the base. The dish is a round flat plate, and the base takes on a trumpet shape. The most eye-catching feature is the squatting mother bear with her cub on the column. The adorable mother bear has a large head with its mouth slightly open. Such lamps with bear designs have been unearthed in regions including Gansu, Shaanxi, Henan, and Ningxia.

The lamps (*deng* in Chinese) in ancient China are believed to have evolved from the food vessel *dou*. The ancient dictionary *Erya* mentions that when made of wood, the vessel is called *dou*; when made of bamboo, it is called *bian*; and when being earthenware, it is called *deng*. Eastern Jin historian Guo Pu (276–324) annotated the last one as "referring to the oil lamp". China has a long history of using lamps as traditional household items, and over thousands of years, various lamp styles have emerged, each with its distinctive characteristics.

The Han dynasty was a vital period for the development of ancient lamps. During this era, lamp designs were unprecedently ingenious and diverse. The main types include *dou*-shaped lamps, shallow dish-shaped lamps, multi-branch lamps, animal-shaped lamps, eared-cup-shaped lamps, *zhi* (wine vessel)-shaped lamps, and lamps with vent pipes. These lamps were often made of pottery, bronze, or iron.

东汉（25 年—220 年）

陶

高 46.50 厘米，口径 16.20 厘米，足径 18.20 厘米

上海博物馆

Eastern Han (25–220)

Green-glazed earthenware

H. 46.50 cm, mouth dia. 16.20 cm, foot dia. 18.20 cm

Shanghai Museum

上海博物馆『百物看中国』文物艺术出境大展系列

CHINA 100: Outbound Exhibition Series of Arts and Cultures

42 | **叠瓣纹樽**
Zun (wine vessel) with Overlapping Petal Pattern

整体为筒形，平口直腹，中腹两侧设铺首衔环耳，下为三虎形足。口部一圈加厚，饰一周菱形云雷纹；上腹部饰四重叠瓣纹；中腹饰二周以粗弦纹为界栏的菱形云雷纹；下腹部饰四重叠瓣纹，和上腹的纹饰形成呼应之势，叠瓣纹下为一周细细的锯齿纹，近底处是一周菱形云雷纹，亦和口部纹饰相呼应。整体造型端庄大气，刻纹细腻生动，十分精巧。

"樽"是出现于战国，盛行于汉代的一种日常实用的盛酒器。汉初开始，随着青铜器的大众化、生活化和由此所带来的实用器类的增多，使得汉代新兴的实用青铜酒器渐渐超越了礼器，从而构成汉代青铜酒器文化发展的基础。

The overall shape of this vessel is cylindrical with a flat mouth and a straight belly. On both sides of the belly are ears with rings, and below are three tiger-shaped feet. The mouth has a thickened rim surrounded by diamond-shaped cloud and thunder patterns. The upper belly bears four layers of overlapping petal patterns. In the middle are two sections of diamond-shaped cloud and thunder patterns separated by a thick string. Another four layers of overlapping petals on the lower belly echo with the upper part, with intricate zigzag patterns beneath. Cloud and thunder patterns repeat near the bottom. The vessel shows a dignified appearance with finely detailed and vivid decorations, displaying exquisite craftsmanship.

The *zun* is a type of daily-use wine vessel that appeared in the Warring States period and became common during the Han dynasty. Starting from the early Han dynasty, with the popularization and commercialization of bronze ware and thus the increase in practical utensils, everyday drinkware gradually superseded ceremonial ones as the mainstream of bronze wine vessels during the Han dynasty.

东汉（25 年—220 年）
铜
高 16.40 厘米，口径 23.40 厘米，深 14.10 厘米
上海博物馆

Eastern Han (25–220)

Bronze

H. 16.40 cm, mouth dia. 23.40 cm, depth. 14.10 cm

Shanghai Museum

43 彩绘云兽纹漆樽（连盖）

Zun (with lid) with Cloud and Animal Pattern

　　木胎。樽呈圆桶形，盖隆起，直壁，平底。盖面边沿有铜朱雀三只，中间嵌柿蒂纹铜饰。器身外壁两旁配铜铺首，底部装铜蹄足三只。樽盖面及外壁通体髹黑漆，朱漆绘云气纹、鸟纹、兽纹等，用几何纹缘边。云纹线条纤细入微，缱绻精致，鸟兽有豺狼、豹、鹿、雀等，穿梭云气之间，或隐或现。

　　盖内朱漆为地，黑漆绘三组云龙纹，龙须髯若藤蔓，身体呈 S 形卷曲，围绕圆钮分布，纤毫毕现。樽内髹朱漆。

　　此樽纹饰繁复，线条细若游丝，内涵丰富。

This *zun* vessel has a wooden body that takes on a cylindrical barrel shape with a raised lid, straight walls, and a flat bottom. Along the edge of the lid are three bronze birds, surrounding a bronze inlay of persimmon calyx motif in the center. On both sides of the vessel are bronze appliques in the shape of animals' heads, and three bronze hoof-shaped feet adorn the bottom. The entire surface and the lid are coated with black lacquer, with intricate patterns of clouds and animals and geometric borders painted in red. Delicate lines illustrate tangled clouds, among which the animals, including jackals, leopards, deer, and sparrows, gracefully roam.

The lid's interior is coated with red lacquer with three sets of cloud and dragon motifs in black colour. The dragons curl in graceful S-shapes around the knob, with their whiskers twining like tendrils, all details revealed. The body's interior is also coated with red lacquer.

The entire design of this vessel boasts complex decorations with rich contents painted in exceptionally fine lines.

西汉（前 206 年—8 年）

漆、木、铜

直径 22.30 厘米，通高 22.50 厘米

上海博物馆

Western Han (206 BCE – 8 CE)

Lacquer, wood, and bronze

Dia. 22.30 cm, overall H. 22.50 cm

Shanghai Museum

44 | 彩绘凤鸟纹漆耳杯
Ear Cup with Phoenix Motif

　　木胎，斫制。耳杯呈椭圆形，口微敛，两侧新月形耳微翘，弧壁，平底。杯内髹朱漆，底部绘凤鸟纹，以黑漆勾画凤鸟的轮廓，再填绿漆。虽寥寥几笔，却生动地表现了凤鸟振翅飞翔的形态。耳部及口沿黑漆地上朱漆绘涡云纹。耳杯外壁及底部髹褐漆，底边髹朱漆一道。

　　汉代彩绘漆器的线条，以纤细为主要特征，往往以凝练的笔触描绘事物的本质。此耳杯线条虽少，却意蕴悠长。

This wooden ear cup takes an oval shape with a slightly tapered mouth, crescent-shaped ears curling on both sides, gently arched walls, and a flat base. The cup's interior is coated with red lacquer, featuring a phoenix motif on the bottom, which is outlined with black lacquer and then filled in green. Simply through a few strokes, it vividly captures the soaring posture of the bird. The ears and the rim are adorned with red whirlwind cloud patterns against a black ground. The exterior walls and the base are coated with brown lacquer, with a red edge along the base.

The distinguishing feature of painted lacquerware in the Han dynasty is its delicate lines that precisely depict the essence of objects. Though minimal, they convey a profound sense of artistry.

西汉（前 206 年—8 年）
漆、木
长 14.60 厘米，宽 10.30 厘米，高 4.20 厘米
上海博物馆

Western Han (206 BCE – 8 CE)
Lacquer and wood
L. 14.60 cm, W. 10.30 cm, H. 4.20 cm
Shanghai Museum

45 | 彩绘鱼纹漆耳杯
Ear Cup with Fish Motif

　　木胎，斫制。耳杯呈椭圆形，口微敛，两侧新月形耳微翘，弧腹，平底。杯内髹朱漆，底部中央绘鱼纹，以黑漆细线条绘的轮廓，用深浅不同的黑漆髹涂鱼的眼睛、眼眶、鳞片、鱼尾等。鱼身修长，似在水中悠游，生趣盎然。耳杯外部及耳部均髹黑漆，质朴简洁。

　　此耳杯与同墓所出的彩绘凤鸟纹漆耳杯风格相似，不施繁复的花纹装饰，仅以寥寥数笔勾勒出杯中游鱼和飞鸟，形虽简，意不绝。

This wooden ear cup takes an oval shape with a slightly tapered mouth, crescent-shaped ears curling on both sides, gently arched walls, and a flat base. The cup's interior is coated with red lacquer, featuring a fish motif on the bottom, which is outlined in black with its eyes, eye sockets, scales, and tail in varied shades of black lacquer. The fish appears slender, as if leisurely swimming in water, exuding a lively and charming quality. The exterior of the ear cup and its ears are coated with black lacquer, exhibiting a simple and unadorned aesthetic.

This ear cup shares a similar style with the cup with a phoenix pattern discovered in the same tomb. Both eschew complex decorations, using only a few strokes to depict the swimming fish or flying birds, simple yet eloquent.

西汉（前 206 年—8 年）

漆、木

长 17.50 厘米，宽 12.50 厘米，高 6.30 厘米

湖北省荆州市高台 28 号汉墓出土

上海博物馆

Western Han (206 BCE – 8 CE)

Lacquer and wood

L. 17.50 cm, W. 12.50 cm, H. 6.30 cm

Excavated from Han-dynasty Tomb M28 at Gaotai, Jingzhou

Shanghai Museum

46 彩绘龙纹立雕人像漆耳杯
Ear Cup with Dragon Pattern and Human Figurine

木胎。耳杯呈椭圆形，口微敛，两侧新月形耳微翘，弧壁，平底。一耳圆雕跽坐侍者，头戴纱冠，着交领袍服。

杯内以黑漆细绘龙纹。龙体轮廓用黑漆勾勒，头、身、足、尾关键部位填绿漆。龙身周围黑漆涡云纹按一定规律分布。杯底中央绘四瓣花卉。杯耳与外壁髹褐漆，耳部朱漆绘云纹、几何纹。外壁朱漆绘水禽纹、涡云纹，底髹黑漆。

此杯构图灵活，最大特点是一耳增添了立体人像，形象生动，既有装饰性又增强了实用功能（可以当把柄使用），创意独特。

This wooden ear cup takes an oval shape with a slightly tapered mouth, crescent-shaped ears curling on both sides, gently arched walls, and a flat base. On one ear is a round-carved figurine sitting on his knees, wearing a gauze hat and a robe with a cross-collar.

The cup's interior features a dragon outlined in black, with its head, body, limbs, and tail filled with green lacquer. Black whirlwind patterns are evenly distributed around the dragon's body. In the center of the bottom is a four-petaled floral motif. The cup's ears and exterior are coated with brown lacquer. The ears are adorned with red clouds and geometric patterns, while the exterior features depictions of waterfowl and whirlwind patterns in red. The base is coated with black lacquer.

This cup has a dynamic composition. Its most distinctive feature – the three-dimensional figurine on one of the ears – is a vivid and unique design that combines both decorative and practical elements as it can be used as a handle.

西汉（前 206 年—8 年）

漆、木

长 12.80 厘米，宽 11.50 厘米，通高 8.40 厘米

上海博物馆

Western Han (206 BCE – 8 CE)

Lacquer and wood

L. 12.80 cm, W. 11.50 cm, overall H. 8.40 cm

Shanghai Museum

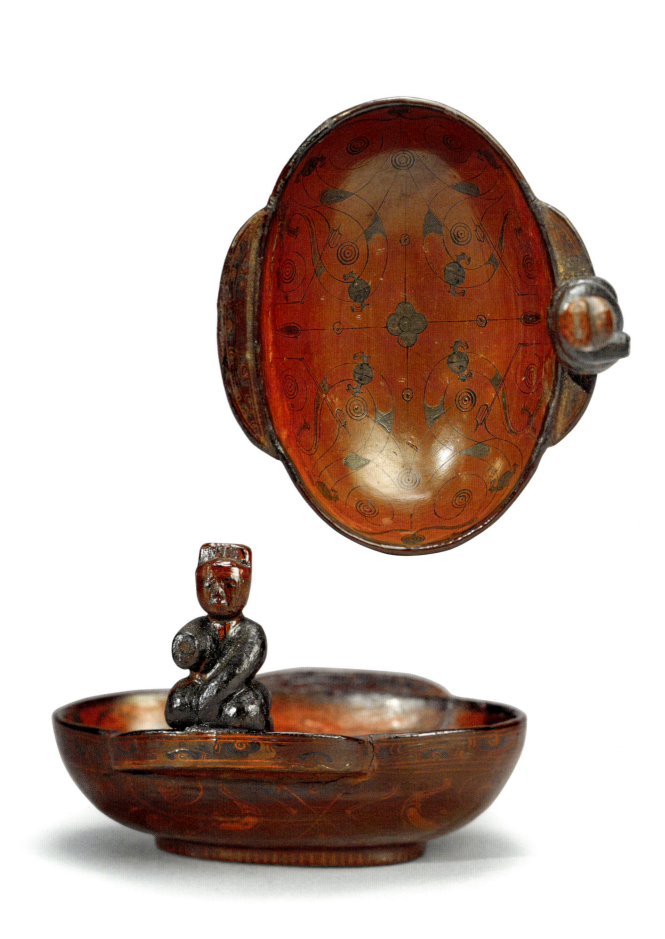

上海博物馆「百物看中国」文物艺术出境大展系列

CHINA 100: Outbound Exhibition Series of Arts and Cultures

47 彩绘云鸟纹漆耳杯（一对）

Ear Cups with Cloud and Bird Pattern (a pair)

木胎。口呈椭圆形，微敛，两侧新月形耳微上翘，弧腹，平底。耳杯内侧髹朱漆，内底中央以褐漆为地，边缘朱绘两圈细弦纹，弦纹内用朱漆绘轮廓，绿漆填涂绘卷云纹。杯外壁、耳、口沿为褐漆地。外壁褐漆地上朱漆绘鸟纹四组，两两相背，鸟翅首细喙，轮廓纤细。耳部以朱漆绘细弦纹，两两相交呈新月形，弦纹内以朱色、绿色漆绘云纹，耳侧亦然。底部髹褐漆，足边缘朱绘细弦纹。

The two wooden ear cups have an oval-shaped, slightly tapered mouth with crescent-shaped ears curling on both sides, gently arched walls, and a flat base. The interior is coated with red lacquer, and the center of the bottom has a brown background with two red concentric circles along the edge. The swirling cloud patterns inside are outlined in red and filled with green lacquer.

Each cup's exterior, ears, and mouth rim are covered in brown lacquer. The exterior features four pairs of back-to-back birds in red. The birds have slender necks and thin beaks. The red lines on the ears from crescent shapes where they intersect. Within these strings, both red and green lacquer are used to paint cloud patterns, which are also found on the back of the ears. The base of the cups is coated in brown lacquer, with string patterns painted in red along the edges.

西汉（前 206 年—8 年）

漆、木

（1）长 12.50 厘米，宽 9.80 厘米，高 4.00 厘米
（2）长 12.50 厘米，宽 9.80 厘米，高 4.00 厘米

上海博物馆

Western Han (206 BCE – 8 CE)

Lacquer and wood

(1) L. 12.50 cm, W. 9.80 cm, H. 4.00 cm
(2) L. 12.50 cm, W. 9.80 cm, H. 4.00 cm

Shanghai Museum

48 | 彩绘云纹漆圆盘
Plate with Cloud Pattern

　　木胎。盘呈圆形，平沿，浅腹。盘内中央为褐漆地，朱绘一道粗弦纹将其分为两区。内区绘鸟纹，鸟喙尖尖，冠羽飘扬，周围饰卷云纹。外区则朱绘一圈变形鱼纹。盘腹髹朱漆。盘边、外壁、口沿均以褐漆为地。盘内边朱漆绘变形鸟头纹（BI 纹）五组，用细弦纹连接。口沿朱绘波折纹间点纹。外壁则朱绘一圈细弦纹与变形鸟纹。外底边沿朱绘弦纹一圈。

　　此盘纹饰布局新颖，鸟纹与云纹、鱼纹与波折纹结合，使得盘面生机盎然。

This wooden plate has a round shape with a flat rim and a shallow cavity. In the center of the interior is a brown lacquer background, divided into two sections by a thick line in red. The inner section features bird motifs with sharp beaks and flowing plumage, surrounded by swirling clouds. The outer section is adorned with a circle of modified fish patterns in red. The belly of the plate is coated with red lacquer.

The plate's rim, exterior, and mouth are covered in brown lacquer. Along the inner edge of the plate, five sets of bird head motifs are painted in red lacquer and connected by lines. The mouth rim features red wavy patterns and dots in between. On the exterior is a red line with modified bird motifs. Another red line decorates the outer edge of the base.

The plate's decoration boasts an innovative layout, combining bird motifs with cloud patterns, and fish motifs with wavy patterns, creating a lively and dynamic design.

西汉（前 206 年—8 年）
漆、木
口径 22.50 厘米，高 3.50 厘米
上海博物馆

Western Han (206 BCE – 8 CE)
Lacquer and wood
Mouth dia. 22.50 cm, H. 3.50 cm
Shanghai Museum

49

彩绘云纹漆盆
Basin with Cloud Pattern

纻胎。盆呈圆形，平沿，侈口，斜壁，折腹，饼底。口沿镶银钿。通体髹黑漆，用朱漆彩绘。盆内底中央略凹，朱绘云气纹满布盆底。其外绘弦纹两道，内绘菱形纹四组。盆内外壁、腹部亦绘云气纹。盆外近底朱漆弦纹一道，底部朱漆隶书"西刘"二字。

汉代漆器中有铭文者较为多见，铭文的内容多种多样：可以是漆器所有者的姓名、制作者的姓名，也可以是制作的工序、产地、督造官员的职位等。此件银钿漆器规格较高，"西刘"铭文未见发表，值得研究者关注。

This linen–body basin has a round shape with a flat rim, a slightly flared mouth, sloping walls, a folded belly, and a flat base. The rim is inlaid with a silver band. The entire body is coated with black lacquer and decorated with red lacquer. The center of the basin's interior is slightly concave, featuring a full spread of cloud patterns painted in red lacquer. Surrounding the center part are two circles, with four sets of diamond-shaped patterns in between. Cloud patterns are also painted on the inner and outer walls and the belly of the basin. Near the base of the basin's exterior is a red line, and on the base there are two characters 西刘 (*Xi Liu*) written in clerical script with red lacquer.

On Han dynasty lacquerware, inscriptions are quite common and vary in content, including the owner's name, the artisan's name, details about the manufacturing process, the place of production, and the title of overseeing officials. This piece with a silver band exhibits a remarkable level of craftsmanship, and there is still a lot to learn about the inscription of *Xi Liu*, making it a noteworthy subject for future study.

西汉（前 206 年—8 年）

漆、布、银

口径 25.00 厘米，高 6.00 厘米

上海博物馆

Western Han (206 BCE – 8 CE)

Lacquer, linen, and silver

Mouth dia. 25.00 cm, H. 6.00 cm

Shanghai Museum

上海博物馆『百物看中国』文物艺术出境大展系列

CHINA 100: Outbound Exhibition Series of Arts and Cultures

西汉（前 206 年—8 年）

漆、木

长 10.80 厘米，宽 8.50 厘米，高 13.20 厘米

上海博物馆

Western Han (206 BCE – 8 CE)

Lacquer and wood

L. 10.80 cm, W. 8.50 cm, H. 13.20 cm

Shanghai Museum

50 彩绘云纹龙头勺

Ladle with Cloud Pattern and Dragon-head-shaped Handle

木胎。勺呈半圆形，长柄。柄部雕龙首，口内衔珠，龙身下展为勺。勺内髹朱漆，以绿、黄、褐等色漆绘云气纹，状似藤蔓，自由流淌，颇为柔美。勺内壁近口沿处绘锯齿纹一圈，以黄漆勾勒，填绿、褐漆。勺外部漆皮剥落，仅见少许黑漆、朱漆、黄漆痕迹，推测原亦绘云纹。

此勺设计巧妙，龙头雕刻生动，云纹姿势曼妙，尽管残损，却仍不失为集实用性与观赏性于一体的漆器佳作。

This wooden ladle has a semi-circular shape with a long handle. The handle is carved into a dragon's head with a pearl in its mouth, its body extending down. The interior of the ladle is coated with red lacquer and adorned with cloud patterns in colours like green, yellow, and brown, resembling rambling vines in a graceful appearance. On the inside of the bowl's rim is a ring of sawtooth patterns outlined in yellow and filled with green and brown lacquer. The exterior of the ladle has suffered some lacquer loss, leaving only few traces of black, red, and yellow lacquer, which suggests that it may have originally featured cloud patterns as well.

Despite its damage, this ladle exhibits clever design with its vividly carved dragon head and graceful cloud patterns. It remains a remarkable lacquerware piece that combines practicality and aesthetics.

51 | 彩绘漆椭圆盒
Oval Box

　　木胎。盒呈椭圆形，盖隆起，直壁，饼底。由套盖与器身上下套合而成。盖顶部分成三区，每一区高度逐层递减。盖外及器身外壁和底部均髹黑漆，用朱、褐漆彩绘。盖顶中央绘卷云纹，纹饰流畅，外层两圈则以朱漆绘小云纹、菱形纹，纹饰间以朱漆弦纹作间隔。盖壁以四道朱弦纹分隔成三区，上下两区内交错绘卷云纹，舒朗优美。器外壁底部亦绘小云纹与菱形纹。器内髹朱漆。

　　此盒器型雅致，制作精巧，较为少见，或为成套漆奁中的一件子奁。

This wooden box is oval-shaped with a raised lid, straight walls, and a flat base. The top of the lid has three layers, with each layer decreasing in height. The exterior of the lid, the outer walls of the body, and the base are coated with black lacquer and decorated with red and brown lacquer. In the center of the lid's top are flowing cloud patterns, surrounded by two tracks of small cloud patterns and diamond-shaped patterns in red lacquer, with red lines in between. The lid's walls contain three sections divided by four red lines, with the upper and lower sections bearing stretching, staggered cloud patterns. The lower reaches of the body's walls also features small clouds and diamond patterns. The interior of the body is coated with red lacquer.

This box, as a rarity, has an elegant design and exquisite craftsmanship, possibly being the smaller one of a certain nest of lacquer boxes.

西汉（前 206 年—8 年）

漆、木

长 17.00 厘米，宽 7.30 厘米，高 8.20 厘米

湖北省荆州市岳桥 62 号汉墓出土

上海博物馆

Western Han (206 BCE – 8 CE)

Lacquer and wood

L. 17.00 cm, W. 7.30 cm, H. 8.20 cm

Excavated from Han-dynasty Tomb M62 at Yueqiao, Jingzhou

Shanghai Museum

上海博物馆『百物看中国』文物艺术出境大展系列

CHINA 100: Outbound Exhibition Series of Arts and Cultures

52 | ## 漆陶鼎

Ding (food vessel)

出土于成都天回镇老官山汉代木椁墓。陶胎，子口，口沿外侧有两个直立附耳，腹较浅直，大圆底近平，兽蹄形矮足。系在陶器表面涂黑色漆为地，用红漆再于上腹部、足跟、足尖、耳外、耳侧等部位绘出花纹。纹饰有平行线纹、水波纹、条带纹、涡云纹、弦纹等。

This piece was unearthed from a wooden coffin in a Han dynasty tomb in Laoguanshan, Tianhui Town, Chengdu. It is made of pottery and features a narrow mouth with two upright attached ears on the outer side. The body is shallow and straight, with a flat, circular base and squat feet resembling animal hooves. The surface is coated with black lacquer, upon which red lacquer depicts various patterns on the upper belly, feet, ears, and other areas. These patterns include parallel lines, water ripple patterns, strips, whirlwind patterns, and string patterns.

西汉（前 206 年—8 年）

漆、陶

口径 18.20 厘米，腹径 26.10 厘米，通高 18.50 厘米

2012 年出土于成都天回镇老官山汉墓

成都文物考古研究院

Western Han (206 BCE – 8 CE)

Lacquer and earthenware

Mouth dia. 18.20 cm, belly dia. 26.10 cm, overall H. 18.50 cm

Excavated from the Han-dynasty tombs at Laoguanshan,

Tianhui Town, Chengdu, in 2012

Chengdu Institute of Archaeology

53 | 漆陶器盖
Lid

西汉（前 206 年—8 年）

漆、陶

直径 20.50 厘米，高 6.70 厘米

2012 年出土于成都天回镇老官山汉墓

成都文物考古研究院

Western Han (206 BCE – 8 CE)

Lacquer and earthenware

Dia. 20.50 cm, H. 6.70 cm

Excavated from the Han-dynasty tombs at Laoguanshan,

Tianhui Town, Chengdu, in 2012

Chengdu Institute of Archaeology

出土于成都天回镇老官山汉代木椁墓，为漆陶鼎的盖。陶胎，圆形，弧顶，顶部有三个圆形凸起，器表髹黑漆，边缘及凸起处涂朱，表面用红彩描绘卷云纹等纹饰。

This lid, originally belonging to a lacquered pottery *ding* (food vessel), was unearthed from a wooden coffin in a Han dynasty tomb in Laoguanshan, Tianhui Town, Chengdu. It has a curved top with three circular protrusions. The surface of the lid is coated with black lacquer, accentuated by edges and protrusions in red lacquer, featuring swirling cloud patterns in red.

上海博物馆『百物看中国』文物艺术出境大展系列

CHINA 100: Outbound Exhibition Series of Arts and Cultures

54 | **鎏金虎镇**
Tiger-shaped Mat Weight

整体为卧虎形，昂首，口微张，长尾弯卷，身躯刻有虎斑花纹。虎颈戴一项圈，饰以贝纹，近后脑处设有半圆环。整体鎏金。

在秦汉及其之前，人们主要的起居方式是"席地而坐"。为了避免起身落座时折卷席角或牵挂衣饰，从而影响仪态，出现了席镇，即压席四角的重物。西汉时期，席镇的使用及制作达到了鼎盛时期，成为汉代室内陈设的亮点。西汉席镇多动物造型，这些席镇制作精美，构思巧妙，体现了汉人的匠心独具，代表了西汉时期手工业的发展水平。

This mat weight takes on the shape of a couchant tiger with a raised head, a slightly open mouth, a curled long tail, and a body adorned with stripes. The tiger wears a collar embellished with shell patterns, and there is a semicircular ring near the back of its head. The entire piece is gilded.

Before and in the Qin and Han dynasties, the Chinese used to sit on the floor. To prevent sitting mats from curling or snagging on clothing, mat weights were introduced to anchor the corners. During the Western Han, mat weights reached their peak in usage and production, becoming a highlight of indoor decor. Many of the mat weights from the Western Han period feature animal designs, showcasing impressive skill and creativity, reflecting the ingenuity of the Han people and representing the high level of craftsmanship during the Western Han period.

东汉（25 年—220 年）
铜
长 17.20 厘米，高 10.40 厘米
上海博物馆

Eastern Han (25–220)
Gilded bronze
L. 17.20 cm, H. 10.40 cm
Shanghai Museum

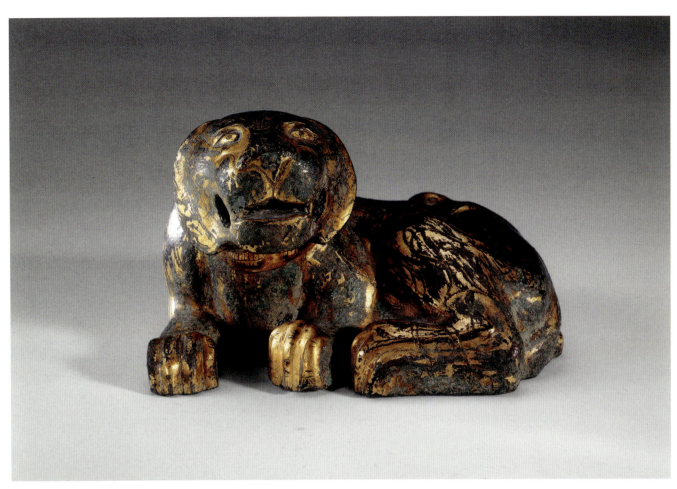

55 鎏金神人神兽画像镜

Mirror with Divine Figures and Mythological Beasts

圆钮，圆形钮座，钮座外围围绕短弧线和相间排列的连珠纹。内区纹饰以四只神兽为间隔，兽头部作高浮雕，主神端坐其间，侍者侧坐在主神右边，神人均有羽翼。外区有相间的凸起半圆和方块枚，半圆块上装饰有云气纹，方块枚上皆有"天王日月"四字，外圈有凸起的锯齿纹和双线纹。镜缘纹饰分为两圈，内圈为六龙驾云车，车上有神人，还有羽人驾青鸟、神兽等图案；外圈饰云气纹。通体鎏金。

在汉代，铜镜迎来了发展高峰，铜镜纹饰蔚为大观，草叶纹、星辰纹、连弧纹、博局纹、龙虎纹、神兽纹以及神仙人物纹等形成了独特的汉代铜镜纹饰。

This mirror has a round knob and a circular knob base surrounded by short arcs and alternating rows of bead patterns. The inner area bears four mythological beasts as intervals, with their heads in high relief. The main deity sits in the center, with an attendant seated to the right, and all divine figures have wings. The outer area has alternating raised semicircles and square pieces, with cloud patterns on the semicircles, and all square pieces bear the characters 天王日月 (*tianwang ri yue*, "Heavenly King, Sun, Moon"). The outermost circle features raised sawtooth patterns and double lines. The patterns on the mirror edge are divided into two sections: the inner track depicts six dragons pulling a chariot with divine figures, winged figures riding on mythical birds, and mythological creatures; the outer circle is filled with cloud patterns. The entire piece is gilded.

During the Han dynasty, bronze mirrors prevailed with a wide variety of decorations, such as grass and leaf patterns, star patterns, curved lines, TLV symbols (motifs of the *liubo* boardgame), dragon and tiger motifs, mythological beasts, and divine figures, forming a distinctive Han dynasty style of bronze mirrors.

东汉（25年—220年）

铜

直径 15.30 厘米

上海博物馆

Eastern Han (25–220)

Bronze

Dia. 15.30 cm

Shanghai Museum

上海博物馆『百物看中国』文物艺术出境大展系列

CHINA 100: Outbound Exhibition Series of Arts and Cultures

56 | 青羊龙虎镜
Mirror with Dragon and Tiger

圆钮，圆形钮座，大钮高凸。镜背纹饰分为内外两区，内区主题纹饰为一龙一虎夹镜钮对峙，上为一虎，下为一龙，龙虎对峙而啸，龙、虎身体与足部充满动感，部分躯体压在钮座下，两者尾部有铭文"青羊为志"。外区纹饰与内区纹饰间饰一周栉齿纹，外区一周锯齿纹，一周双线波折纹，中间以弦纹相隔。

龙虎镜是中国古代青铜镜文化中的一个重要分类。龙虎镜以巧妙的构思、精湛的艺术和美好的意蕴在东汉时期大为流行，往往采用高浮雕技法，使得龙虎形态活灵活现。

This mirror has a prominently raised large, round knob and a circular knob base. The back design is divided into two areas, inner and outer. In the inner area, the central theme depicts a dragon and a tiger confronting each other around the knob with dynamic bodies and limbs. Some parts of their bodies are hidden beneath the knob base, and there are inscriptions near their tails that read 青羊为志 (*qingyang wei zhi*, "made the inscription on this green auspiciousness"). Between the inner and outer areas is a ring of vertical lines followed by zigzag patterns in the outer area, and then another circle of double-lined wavy patterns, separated by a string.

The mirror with the dragon and tiger motif is an important category in ancient Chinese bronze mirror culture. During the Eastern Han period, it became widely popular for its ingenious design, exquisite artistry, and profound symbolism. The motif often shows in high relief, bringing the dragon and tiger to life.

东汉（25 年—220 年）

铜

直径 10.00 厘米

上海博物馆

Eastern Han (25–220)

Bronze

Dia. 10.00 cm

Shanghai Museum

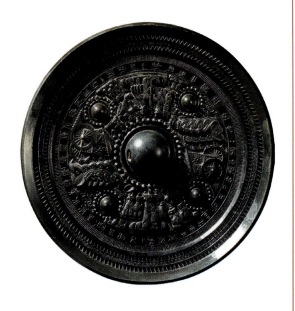

东汉（25 年—220 年）

铜

直径 21.30 厘米

上海博物馆

Eastern Han (25–220)

Bronze

Dia. 21.30 cm

Shanghai Museum

57 吴向里车马画像镜

Mirror with Chariots and Horses

圆钮凸起较高，圆形钮座，钮座外围饰实心连珠纹。内区纹饰以周饰实心连珠纹的四枚为界，有两组对称的神人和车马，纹饰为浮雕。内区纹饰外围有一圈铭文："吴向里柏氏作竟（镜），四夷服，多贺国家人民息，胡虏殄灭天下复，风雨时节五谷熟，长保二亲得天力，传告后世乐无极兮。"铭文外围饰一周栉齿纹，外区纹饰有三圈：从内而外分别是锯齿纹、双线波折纹、锯齿纹。

画像镜是以浮雕技法表现神仙羽人、神禽瑞兽、历史人物、车马、屋舍等纹饰题材的一个特殊镜种，以绍兴出土最多，主要流行于东汉中后期，至三国时期衰微。此类镜内容丰富、雕琢精致、形体较大，具有强烈的立体感和生动的视觉效果，在中国铜镜发展史中别具一格，具有重要的历史价值与艺术价值。

This mirror has a round, high knob and a circular knob base with the outer edge decorated with a row of beads. In the inner area, delimited by four beads, are two symmetrical depictions of divine figures, chariots, and horses in relief. The surrounding inscription mentions the artisan surnamed Bai from the Wu county. Next is a ring of vertical lines. The outer area features three concentric circles: zigzag patterns, double-lined wavy patterns, and zigzags again.

Mirrors with depictions of scenes are a distinctive type of mirror characterized by their subjects in relief, such as divine beings, winged humans, auspicious creatures, historical figures, chariots, horses, and buildings, mostly excavated from Shaoxing, Zhejiang province. They were prevalent during the middle to late Eastern Han period, gradually declining during the Three Kingdoms period (220–280). These mirrors are known for their rich content, intricate carvings, large size, and vivid three-dimensional visual effects. They hold significant historical and artistic value for the development of Chinese bronze mirrors.

58 | 彩绘云兽纹六子漆奁

Seven-pack Nested *Lian* (cosmetic boxes) with Cloud and Animal Pattern

纻胎。由母奁和六件子奁套合而成，六件子奁分别为两件圆形、两件方形、一件长方形、一件马蹄形。奁盖顶部中心皆嵌有柿蒂纹银片，银片形状随奁的形状而变。奁均以褐漆为地，用朱漆、灰绿漆彩绘。母奁盖面绘云纹、菱形纹、鹿纹等，鹿纹间夹四组兽形银片。母奁外壁满绘云气纹、兽纹，有猴子、鹿、豺狼等，诸兽穿梭于云气之间，纹饰自然飘逸。子奁则绘云气纹。奁内髹朱漆。

奁又名"镜奁""镜匣""妆盒"等，汉代十分流行。东汉许慎的《说文解字》对奁的解释是："奁，镜奁也。"由此可见奁的作用是用以盛镜子、脂粉等梳妆用品。汉代的多子奁往往以一个母奁中置多个子奁的形式出现，子奁多三子、五子、七子等奇数，六子奁则较为少见。

西汉（前 206 年—8 年）

漆、布、银

（1）大圆奁：径 23.60 厘米，高 11.40 厘米

（2）圆盒：径 7.90 厘米，高 6.40 厘米

（3）小圆盒：径 6.20 厘米，高 5.70 厘米

（4）方盒：宽 7.00 厘米，高 6.40 厘米

（5）小方盒：宽 5.50 厘米，高 6.40 厘米

（6）长方盒：长 12.70 厘米，宽 5.20 厘米，高 6.40 厘米

（7）马蹄形盒：长 8.00 厘米，宽 6.30 厘米，高 6.40 厘米

上海博物馆

Western Han (206 BCE – 8 CE)

Lacquer, linen, and silver

(1) Large round box: Dia. 23.60 cm, H. 11.40 cm

(2) Medium round box: Dia. 7.90 cm, H. 6.40 cm

(3) Small round box: Dia. 6.20 cm, H. 5.70 cm

(4) Large square box: W. 7.00 cm, H. 6.40 cm

(5) Small square box: W. 5.50 cm, H. 6.40 cm

(6) Rectangular box: L. 12.70 cm, W. 5.20 cm, H. 6.40 cm

(7) Hoof-shaped box: L. 8.00 cm, W. 6.30, cm H.6.40 cm

Shanghai Museum

This set of linen–body boxes consists of a main box and six nested boxes: two round, two square, one rectangular, and one hoof-shaped. Each lid of the boxes is embedded with silver persimmon calyx motifs, the form of which varies according to the shape of the box. The boxes are coated with brown lacquer and decorated with red and greyish-green lacquer. The main box lid is adorned with cloud patterns, diamond patterns, and deer motifs, with four sets of animal-shaped silver pieces between the deer motifs. The outer walls of the main box are covered with cloud and animal patterns, featuring monkeys, deer, and jackals, which roam through the clouds, creating a natural and elegant appearance. The other six nested boxes feature cloud patterns, with the interior coated in red lacquer.

The *lian* was prevalent during the Han dynasty. According to Eastern Han scholar Xu Shen's *Shuowen Jiezi (An Explication of Written Characters)*, the term *lian* refers to a box with a mirror, indicating that these boxes were used to store mirrors, cosmetics, and other grooming items. Nested cosmetic boxes from the Han dynasty commonly come in four, six, or eight packs. Sets of seven are rare.

59 | 绿釉陶兽纹奁

Lian with Animal Pattern

　　红陶胎，外施铅绿釉，釉色青绿透明。器外壁模印纹饰，表现的是各种动物出没于山川之间，其中体型较大的是两头狮子，另外还有螭龙、奔鹿、游鸭等等。此器带盖，为博山形盖，高耸的山峦之间也有动物出没。底承以三足，为三个憨态可掬的小熊。

　　奁最早出现于西周时期，汉魏六朝时期最为流行，中原汉墓中有大量出土，多为铅绿釉或黄釉陶器。而奁的用途，一般认为是古代盛放梳妆用具的器皿，《说文解字》亦称其为"镜奁"。而另有学者认为其用途应是作温酒之用。

This *lian* has a red clay body, coated in transparent green lead glaze, which appears as a clear bluish-green color. The exterior of the vessel is decorated with molded patterns depicting various animals amid mountains and rivers. Among them, the larger ones are two lions, and there are also *chi*-dragons (hornless dragons), galloping deer, and swimming ducks. This vessel comes with a lid in the shape of the mythical Boshan Mountain, also with animals amidst the peaks. The base is supported by three legs, each resembling a cute little bear.

Lian first appeared during the Western Zhou period and became particularly popular from the Han through the Southern and Northern Dynasties (420–589). Many were unearthed from Han tombs in the Central Plains, mostly green lead-glazed or yellow-glazed earthenware. The *lian* is generally believed to be a cosmetics container. According to Eastern Han scholar Xu Shen's *Shuowen Jiezi* (*An Explication of Written Characters*), the term *lian* refers to a box with a mirror, while some suggest it may have been used for warming wine.

汉（前 206 年—220 年）

陶

连盖高 27.60 厘米，腹径 22.30 厘米

上海博物馆

Han (206 BCE – 220 CE)

Earthenware

H. (with lid) 27.60 cm, belly dia. 22.30 cm

Shanghai Museum

60 | 玉带钩
Belt Hook

西汉（前 206 年—8 年）

玉

长 7.20 厘米，宽 1.10 厘米，高 1.10 厘米

2004 年出土于徐州大孤山 M2

徐州博物馆

Western Han (206 BCE – 8 CE)

Jade

L. 7.20 cm, W. 1.10 cm, H. 1.10 cm

Excavated from Tomb M2 at Dagushan, Xuzhou, in 2004

Xuzhou Museum

青白玉，表面有白色沁斑。鸭首状钩首，钩身为弧形，蘑菇形钮，钮面椭圆形。玉质带钩盛行于战国时期，它是人们用在腰带上的饰品，起扣拢腰带的作用，故名带钩，带钩有以铜、铁、玉等多种材料制成，带钩古时又名"师比"。

This piece of greenish-white jade, with white mottling of alteration on its surface, features a duck-head-shaped curved hook and a mushroom-shaped button with an oval panel. The use of jade belt hooks dates back to the Warring States period (746–221 BCE) as a decorative accessory worn on the waist to fasten or tighten the belt. Belt hooks were made from various materials, including bronze, iron, and jade, and were also referred to as *shibi* in ancient China.

61 | 蝉纹带钩
Belt Hook with Cicada

　　带钩整体为写实的蝉形。钩首上卷，钩颈光素无纹，可见中部隆起的脊线，钩面蝉圆鼓，双目凸出，两长翼延伸为钩尾，两长翼间有一似长三角形孔洞。钩背内凹，钮柱较短，钮面稍宽。整体线条较为流畅。

　　带钩是古代扣接束腰革带及别在腰带上悬挂囊物、装饰品的钩，也是佩戴者身份地位的重要标识，最早可追溯至 4000 年前良渚文化时期的玉带钩。东周秦汉时期，带钩使用最为普及，其使用及影响渗透到了古代社会生活的许多方面。

This belt hook takes the realistic form of a cicada. The hook's tip curls upwards, and the neck is plain without patterns, revealing a raised ridge line in the middle. The cicada is rounded and swollen, with protruding eyes, and its two long wings extend into the hook's end, with a triangular-shaped hole in between. The back is concave, the button column short, and the panel is slightly wider. The overall design features smooth lines.

Belt hooks were fasteners used to secure leather belts and to hang bags and ornaments on the waist. They were also important indicators of the wearer's social status and identity. The emergence of jade belt hooks can be traced back to the Liangzhu Culture period, approximately 4,000 years ago. During the Eastern Zhou, Qin, and Han periods, belt hooks became widely popular. The saying "Stealing a state makes one a noble, while stealing a belt hook leads to execution" from the book *Zhuangzi* demonstrates their significant roles in many aspects of society and life.

汉（前 206 年—220 年）

铜

长 6.80 厘米

上海博物馆

Han (206 BCE – 220 CE)

Bronze

L. 6.80 cm

Shanghai Museum

62 伎乐人物带钩

Belt Hook with Musicians

钩身上三伎乐席地而坐，左边的弹奏者宽衣大袖，双手正在拨弄琴弦，琴略呈矩形，上面横向装饰的五根凸弦纹，细致地刻画了琴弦；右侧的人物似在吹竽，精细地刻画出弹琴述怀的情趣。琴身的右侧延伸出长钩，钩首可见兽头装饰，背面有一伞状扣钮，以连缀革带。此伎乐人物带钩形象别致，结构精巧，是青铜艺术品中的佳作。

内蒙古准格尔旗瓦尔吐沟出土过类似的三伎乐铜带钩。汉代强盛的国力和丰富的物质生活，促使礼乐大兴，这件抚琴伎乐人物带钩就是这种礼兴乐盛的集中体现，生动地再现了汉代礼乐文化的繁荣景象。

The hook depicts three musicians sitting on the floor. The musician on the left, wearing a wide robe with large sleeves, is playing a rectangular-shaped *qin* (zither), which is intricately adorned with five raised strings. The figure on the right appears to be playing the *yu* (reed instrument). Their expressive postures beautifully capture the enjoyment of playing music. The hook extends from the right side, with an animal head decoration at the tip. On the back is an umbrella-shaped button for connecting the belt. This belt hook with musicians is unique in appearance, finely crafted, and represents a masterpiece in ancient Chinese bronze art.

Similar bronze belt hooks featuring musicians have been unearthed in Jungar Banner of Inner Mongolia. During the Han dynasty, the country's strength and prosperous material life led to a flourishing culture of ritual and music. This belt hook serves as a remarkable representation of this cultural blossoming, vividly illustrating the thriving music culture of the Han dynasty.

汉（前 206 年—220 年）

铜

长 5.20 厘米

上海博物馆

Han (206 BCE – 220 CE)

Bronze

L. 5.20 cm

Shanghai Museum

63 | **傩神带钩**
Belt Hook with Nuo God

　　带钩钩身主体为傩神，其头部长出粗壮的顶角，与长钩融为一体，钩首作兽首形。傩神怒目圆睁，微微翘起的两鬓毛发从耳部向下延伸至肩部，发丝根根分明。身穿鳞片饰衣物，左手执盾，右手执一匕。腿部盘曲，身下似乎还有一手，执一兵器，背面一钮，以连革带。

　　傩原系我国古代腊月举行的一种驱逐疫鬼的仪式，如《吕氏春秋·季冬》载"命有司祭大傩"，高诱注："大傩，逐尽阴气为阳导也，今人腊岁前一日击鼓驱疫，谓之逐除是也。"傩神的崇拜流行于现今巴蜀、渝东、湘西等地。

The belt hook features a Nuo god, with a thick horn extending from its head, seamlessly merging with the hook, the tip of which resembles an animal's head. The god has wide-open, angry eyes and slightly raised hair reaching down from the ears to the shoulders, with each strand clearly defined. The god is dressed in scale-patterned garments, holding a shield in the left hand and a dagger in the right. The legs are crossed, and beneath the figure appears to be another hand holding a weapon. On the back is a button for connecting the belt.

Originally, Nuo was a ritual in ancient China held in the twelfth lunar month to expel evil spirits. As mentioned in *Master Lü's Spring and Autumn Annals*, the officers were "commanded to perform the grand Nuo ritual". Eastern Han scholar Gao You annotated that the grand Nuo ritual is about "expelling all yin energy and bringing yang energy", and on the day before the lunar new year, "people beat drums to drive away diseases and evils". The worship of Nuo gods was prevalent in regions such as Sichuan, Chongqing, and western Hunan.

汉（前 206 年—220 年）

铜

长 9.10 厘米

上海博物馆

Han (206 BCE – 220 CE)

Bronze

L. 9.10 cm

Shanghai Museum

上海博物馆『百物看中国』文物艺术出境大展系列

CHINA 100: Outbound Exhibition Series of Arts and Cultures

64 | **乐舞百戏画像石**
Relief of *Baixi* (variety show)

东汉（25 年—220 年）

石灰岩

纵 86.50 厘米，横 84.50 厘米，厚 23.00 厘米

上海博物馆

Eastern Han (25–220)

Limestone

L. 86.50 cm, W. 84.50 cm, thickness 23.00 cm

Shanghai Museum

　　画像石采用线刻手法，上部居中为西王母，两侧为侍从，西王母下方立一建鼓，两人敲击，两旁排列一众表演乐舞的人物。下方有多人围观欣赏。画像石四周用几何纹饰装饰。

This relief uses line engraving techniques. In the center of the upper part is the Queen Mother of the West, with attendants on both sides. Below her stands a drum, with two people playing it, flanked by figures performing dance and music. In the lower part, a crowd gathers to watch and enjoy the performance. Geometric patterns decorate the surroundings on the relief.

65 | 抚琴陶俑
Figurine Playing the *Qin* (zither)

泥质灰陶俑，头戴平巾帻，着交领宽袖袍服，置琴于膝上，双手抚琴，神色怡然，颇有陶然忘我之态。

远古多见打击乐及管乐器，弦乐器在春秋、战国时产生，至汉代已十分发达。传世及出土汉俑中，多见演奏弦乐者，有瑟、琴、筝、筑之别，颇易混淆。瑟是弹散音的乐器，一弦一音，调弦后双手并弹，指法多扣、弹，故称鼓瑟，仅当奏变宫、变徵音时需按弦。琴则利用按弦变动弦分，可在一根弦上弹不同音，演奏时左手按弦，右手拨弦，指法多变，习称抚琴。筝和筑也用于奏散音，极少按弦，区别在于筝以手弹，筑以竹尺击弦，故有弹筝击筑之别。此俑左手按弦，右手弹拨，显然是抚琴俑。西汉琴尾尚用实木，东汉工艺改进，共鸣腔已延至琴尾，音量与音色皆有提高，产生了如张道"响泉"、蔡邕"焦尾"等一代名琴。

This grey earthenware figurine wears a flat hat and a wide-sleeved robe with a cross-collar and is playing a musical instrument called a *qin* (zither) on the knees, displaying a serene expression and a sense of immersion in the music.

In ancient times, there were only percussion and wind instruments. Stringed instruments emerged during the Spring and Autumn and the Warring States periods and reached maturity by the Han dynasty. Among the extant and excavated Han dynasty earthen ware figurines, there are many depicting musicians playing stringed instruments, including *se*, *qin*, *zheng*, and *zhu*. Distinguishing these instruments can be challenging. The *se* produces scattered notes, with one string corresponding to one note. When playing the *se*, both hands pluck the strings simultaneously, often involving techniques like slapping and flicking, hence called *guse* ("to hit the *se*"). Only playing alterations requires pressing the strings. The qin, on the other hand, can produce different notes by altering the finger positions on one string. When playing, the left hand presses the strings while the right hand plucks them, with various fingering techniques – a way referred to as *fuqin* ("to stroke the *qin*"). The *zheng* and *zhu* also produce scattered notes, with minimal string pressing. The key difference lies in the playing technique: the *zheng* is played by finger plucking – *tanzheng* ("to pluck the *zheng*"), while the *zhu* requires striking the strings with a bamboo rod – *jizhu* ("to strike the *zhu*"). This figurine depicts a musician playing the qin, as evidenced by the left-hand pressing of the strings and the right-hand plucking. During the Western Han period, *qin* kept a solid wooden tailpiece. By the Eastern Han period, craftsmanship had improved, and the resonating chamber got extended to the tail, leading to increased sound quality and volume. This improvement gave rise to famous exemplars, like musician Zhang Dao's *Xiangquan* ("The Singing Spring") and scholar Cai Yong's *Jiaowei* ("The Burnt Tail").

汉（前 206 年—220 年）

陶

高 32.40 厘米，宽 35.00 厘米

上海博物馆

Han (206 BCE – 220 CE)

Earthenware

H. 32.40 cm, W. 35.00 cm

Shanghai Museum

66 | 吹笛陶俑
Figurine Playing the *Di* (flute)

　　泥质红陶俑，跽坐，着交领窄袖袍服，手执管乐，忘情吹奏，似沉醉于乐声之中，颇得汉俑生动传神之精髓。陶俑所吹之乐器，汉代称作笛，秦汉之笛，可横吹亦可竖吹，不似后世以横吹者为笛，竖吹者为箫。而先秦至汉代所谓箫者皆指排箫，《说文·竹部》："箫，参差管乐，像凤之翼。"可见为乐管编联之排箫。

　　汉代画像石、陶俑中所见乐师形象极多，多成套出现，组合形式多样，丝竹、钟鼓、管弦、金石，不一而足，且常与乐舞、百戏等配合。汉赋中描绘宴饮，亦多见宫廷雅乐与民间俗乐百戏同台演出，既有礼乐教化之功，亦具怡情娱性之乐，呈现出雅俗交融的特点。

This red earthenware figurine sits on his knees, wearing a cross-collared robe with tight sleeves. The musician is playing a wind instrument with great passion, as if completely lost in the music, displaying the essence of the vivid Han dynasty figurines. The musical instrument is referred to as a *di* (flute) during the Han dynasty. During the Qin and Han dynasties, the *di* could be either side-blown or end-blown, while in later eras, *di* refers to transverse flutes and *xiao* as side-blown flutes. In the pre-Qin to Han period, xiao typically referred to pan flutes, as described in the *Shuowen Jiezi (An Explication of Written Characters)* dictionary:"*Xiao*, a multi-tube musical instrument, resembles the wings of a phoenix."

Han dynasty stone reliefs and earthenware figurines often depict various images of musicians in sets with diverse combinations. They play stringed instruments, wind instruments, percussions, drums, and metal and stone musical instruments. These musicians frequently perform alongside dances and other entertainments. In Han dynasty poetry depicting feasts and gatherings, there are many instances of courtly music, folk music, and other shows performed on the same stage. Such performances not only serve educational and cultural purposes but also provide entertainment, reflecting the fusion of high culture and popular culture.

东汉（25 年—220 年）

陶

通高 73.00 厘米，最宽 37.00 厘米，底宽 33.00 厘米

上海博物馆

Eastern Han (25–220)

Earthenware

Overall H. 73.00 cm, max. W. 37.00 cm, base W. 33.00 cm

Shanghai Museum

67 | 俳优俑
Comedian Figurine

出土于成都新川创新科技园。俳优俑，又叫说唱俑，是四川地区汉代墓葬中具有地域特色的随葬器物。泥质陶。陶俑上半身裸体，一手持鼓，一手提裤，正在进行说唱表演。其形体夸张，表情幽默诙谐，反映了当时天府之国富庶安逸，人们积极乐观的精神面貌。

Unearthed from the Singapore-Sichuan Hi-Tech Innovation Park in Chengdu, this figurine belongs to the category of comedian figurines, also known as *shuochang* (a storytelling performing art) figurines, which are a distinctive feature of Han dynasty burial items of the Sichuan region. This earthenware figurine depicts a half-naked performer, with one hand holding a drum and the other holding up pants, engrossed in his storytelling performance. His exaggerated form and humorous expression reflect the prosperity of Chengdu as the "Land of Plenty" and the carefree and optimistic way of life there during the Han dynasty.

东汉（25 年—220 年）

陶

高 59.00 厘米，宽 25.00 厘米，厚 26.00 厘米

2019 年出土于成都新川创新科技园

成都文物考古研究院

Eastern Han (25–220)

Earthenware

H. 59.00 cm, W. 25.00 cm, Thickness 26.00 cm

Excavated from the Singapore-Sichuan Hi-Tech

Innovation Park, Chengdu, in 2019

Chengdu Institute of Archaeology

68 吹笛俑
Figurine Playing the *Di* (flute)

东汉（25 年—220 年）

陶

高 60.00 厘米，宽 40.00 厘米，厚 25.00 厘米

2019 年出土于成都新川创新科技园

成都文物考古研究院

Eastern Han (25–220)

Earthenware

H. 60.00 cm, W. 40.00 cm, thickness 25.00 cm

Excavated from the Singapore-Sichuan Hi-Tech

Innovation Park, Chengdu, in 2019

Chengdu Institute of Archaeology

出土于成都新川创新科技园。泥质灰陶。身着交领袍服，头戴帻，踞坐状，双手持笛，置于唇下，吹奏状，表情平和，笑容自然。

Unearthed from the Singapore-Sichuan Hi-Tech Innovation Park in Chengdu, this grey earthenware figurine is wearing a cross-collared robe and a headdress. The performer sits on his knees, playing a *di* (flute) with both hands holding it to the lips. His expression is serene, and the smile appears natural.

Part III

信仰的光芒

对于长生、永生的追求是不分地域的话题。汉朝先民对宇宙和彼岸的理解玄幻浪漫，利用想象构设出天空四象、飞凤游龙和神仙居所，创造出一个逍遥自在、雄奇多彩的信仰世界。生时，佩玉等以驱疫避邪，企望长生不老、羽化成仙。逝后，以玉塞九窍求尸身不腐，更将生前的屋、买地的券、驯养的家畜、侍奉的奴仆等模制入土，做轮回再归、富贵再拥的梦。

Radiance of Beliefs

The pursuit of longevity and eternal life knows no geographical bounds. The perception of the universe and the afterlife during the Han dynasty was a blend of fantasy and romance. People crafted notions of imaginary guardians of the four cardinal directions, devine animals like dragons and phoenixes, and abodes of immortals, creating a carefree, magnificent, and colourful world of faith. During their lifetimes, people wore jades to ward off evil spirits, aspiring for immortality and transcendence. After their demise, jades were placed to seal the body orifices with the intention of preventing decomposition. Models of houses, land-sale contracts, domesticated animals, and servants accompanied the deceased in the tomb, envisioning a dream of reincarnation and retaining wealth.

69

四灵纹玉胜

Ornament with the Four Holy Beasts

白玉。整器以透雕技法琢饰"四灵"纹样，即青龙、白虎、朱雀、玄武四种具有方位意义的灵兽。隔柱侧视作胜形，浅刻有篆书铭文"长宜子孙，延寿万年"。"四灵"常以较为固定的方阵出现在汉代画像石、壁画、铜镜、陶器等载体上，寓意天下大治、人民安居乐业。

传说中，西王母"豹尾虎齿而善啸，蓬发戴胜"。"胜"可谓西王母的标志性头饰。汉代人因崇拜西王母而流行戴胜，有辟邪压胜、追求长生的寓意。四灵纹样在汉代十分常见，但四灵纹玉胜却十分罕见，体量虽小，却弥足珍贵。

This piece of white jade is intricately carved using the openwork technique with depictions of the Four Holy Beasts, namely the Azure Dragon, White Tiger, Vermilion Bird, and Black Tortoise, which symbolize cardinal directions. From the side view, the columns appear in the shape of *sheng* (dumbbell-shaped headgear). The seal-script inscription engraved on the columns reads: "May your offspring prosper, and your life be extended for eternity." Motifs of the Four Holy Beasts often appear in a fixed composition on various objects from the Han dynasty, such as stone reliefs, murals, bronze mirrors, and earthenware, symbolizing the prosperity of the country and the well-being of its people.

According to legend, the Queen Mother of the West "has a leopard's tail and tiger's teeth, adept at roaring, and wears a *sheng* to pin her untamed hair". The headgear *sheng* had become her distinctive hallmark. The worship of the Queen Mother of the West during the Han dynasty led to the trend of wearing similar ornaments, signifying protection against evil and the pursuit of longevity. While depictions of the Four Holy Beasts were common, jade *sheng*-shaped ornaments featuring these motifs are extremely rare and, despite their small size, highly precious.

东汉（25 年—220 年）

玉

长 5.50 厘米，宽 2.10 厘米，高 3.20 厘米

上海博物馆

Eastern Han (25–220)

Jade

L. 5.50 cm, W. 2.10 cm, H. 3.20 cm

Shanghai Museum

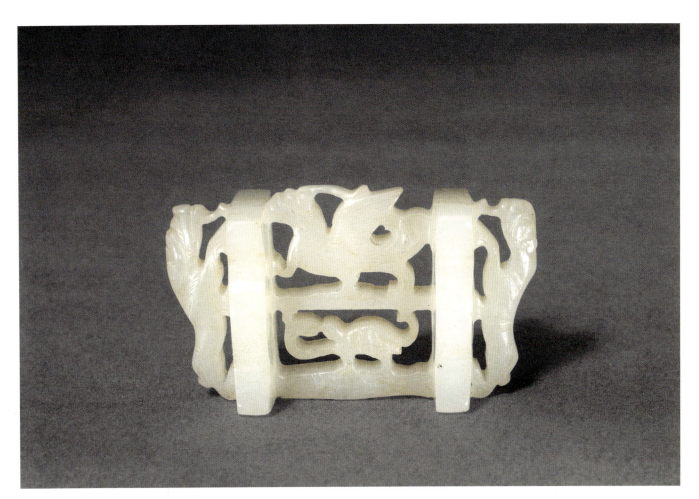

70 | **四灵镜**

Mirror with the Four Holy Beasts

　　圆钮，柿蒂钮座，外围斜线及周圈。外区分置四乳突枚，每组有勾云纹线贯穿其间，每组内饰青龙、白虎、朱雀、玄武。宽缘。

　　"四灵"图像在东汉镜中为常见题材，在西汉镜中却较少。四灵代表四方神灵，在汉代的壁画、帛画、瓦当、印章和画像石上，经常有所反映。关于四灵的内容，在《三辅黄图》上就已指出，为"苍龙、白虎、朱雀、玄武"。而《礼记·礼运》："何谓四灵，麟、凤、龟、龙，谓之四灵。"从大量汉镜上的四灵纹图案来看，汉代四灵为东方青龙、西方白虎、南方朱雀、北方玄武。

This mirror has a round knob and persimmon-calyx-shaped knob base, surrounded by slanting lines and a ring. Four protruding nails divide the outer area into four sections, which feature cloud patterns tangling around the motifs of the Azure Dragon, White Tiger, Vermilion Bird, and Black Tortoise, abutting a broad edge.

The imagery of the Four Holy Beasts was a common subject in Eastern Han mirrors, but less so in the Western Han. The Four Holy Beasts represent the guardians of the four cardinal directions, frequently depicted in Han dynasty murals, silk paintings, roof tiles, seals, and stone reliefs. The four creatures are described in the ancient geography book *Sanfu Huangtu*, while the symbols differ in the *Book of Rites*, including the qilin, phoenix, tortoise, and dragon. According to the motifs in numerous mirrors, the four symbols in the Han dynasty were the Azure Dragon of the east, the White Tiger of the west, the Vermilion Bird of the south, and the Black Tortoise of the north.

西汉（前 206 年—8 年）

铜

直径 15.10 厘米

上海博物馆

Western Han (206 BCE – 8 CE)

Bronze

Dia. 15.10 cm

Shanghai Museum

71 | 玉珩

Heng (arc-shaped pendant)

西汉（前 206 年—8 年）

玉

长 22.80 厘米，宽 4.50 厘米，厚 0.40 厘米

2002 年出土于徐州市九里区天齐山汉墓

徐州博物馆

Western Han (206 BCE – 8 CE)

Jade

L. 22.80 cm, W. 4.50 cm, thickness 0.40 cm

Excavated from a Han tomb at Tianqishan, Xuzhou, in 2004

Xuzhou Museum

青玉。正背两面纹饰相同，两端透雕龙首，中间阴刻兽面。正中顶部有一单面钻穿孔。汉代玉珩常作为握具，为敛葬玉器组合的一部分。从目前资料来看，两端雕龙首的玉珩大部分都属于握具。在徐州地区，珩形玉握基本上都是与玉面罩搭配使用。

This piece of green jade has identical carvings on the front and back sides, with openwork dragon heads carved at both ends and a beast face engraved in the center. At the top center, there is a single-sided drilled hole. In the Han dynasty, the jade *heng* was often used as a grip in a set of jade burial objects. In the Xuzhou region, *heng*-shaped jade grips were typically used together with jade face coverings. Based on existing records, most jade *heng* with dragon heads at both ends served as grips.

72 | **玉珩**

Heng (arc-shaped pendant)

西汉（前 206 年—8 年）

玉

长 23.00 厘米，宽 4.80 厘米，厚 0.50 厘米

2002 年出土于徐州天齐山汉墓

徐州博物馆

Western Han (206 BCE – 8 CE)

Jade

L. 23.00 cm, W. 4.80 cm, Thickness 0.50 cm

Excavated from a Han tomb at Tianqishan, Xuzhou, in 2004

Xuzhou Museum

73 蟠龙玉饰
Coiled Dragon

白玉，局部有赭红色沁。此蟠龙玉饰阴刻一咬尾回转的蟠龙，有循环往复之意。蟠龙卷眉上翘，圆眼宽鼻阔嘴，须发后曳，龙身饰有鳞纹。

龙是中国古代流行的吉祥图案之一。西汉初年，龙成为专制皇权的象征。两汉时期，龙的形象逐渐图像和写意化，较先秦时期更为丰富多彩。环形玉龙于新石器时代凌家滩文化中已可见，西汉此类玉饰多由战国时期造型演变而来，可分为齿尾相扣、唇尾相连等造型，至东汉时期环形玉龙造型更为立体复杂。

This piece of white jade, with reddish-brown alterations, depicts a coiled dragon biting its own tail, symbolizing an eternal cycle. The dragon has an upturned snout, round eyes, wide nostrils, a broad mouth, and trailing whiskers, with fish scale patterns decorating its body.

The dragon is one of the auspicious symbols popular in ancient China and became a symbol of imperial authority in the early Western Han dynasty. During the Han dynasty, the imagery of dragons gradually became more abstract and varied compared to the pre-Qin period. Circular jade dragons have been found in the Lingjiatan Culture of the Neolithic era, and similar jade ornaments from the Western Han period evolved from earlier forms seen in the Warring States period. The dragons can be biting their tails with teeth or touching their tails with lips. The design of circular jade dragons became more complex during the Eastern Han period.

汉（前 206 年—220 年）

玉

长 5.20 厘米，宽 4.25 厘米

上海博物馆

Han (206 BCE – 220 CE)

Jade

L. 5.20 cm, W. 4.25 cm

Shanghai Museum

74 | 龙凤纹韘形玉佩
Thumb-ring-shaped Pendant with Dragon and Phoenix

　　青白玉，局部有赭褐色沁。此龙凤纹韘形玉佩阴刻龙、凤纹，凤鸟圆眼尖喙，以多种阴刻线组合刻划羽翼，线条流畅优美；龙纹须发后曳，龙身盘曲，后肢矫健有力，尾部分叉卷曲。四周装饰有 S 形云纹。

　　韘原是古人拉弓射箭时套于拇指便于勾弦的实用器，早期兼具实用、装饰及身份象征意义。战国中期以后，随着西周"射礼"的世俗化，实用型玉韘逐渐式微，演变为韘形玉佩。

This piece of greenish-white jade pedant, with reddish-brown alterations, features anarcher's-ring shape intricately engraved with a dragon and a phoenix. The phoenix has round eyes and a pointed beak, with its feathers skillfully engraved in smooth, graceful lines. The dragon, with trailing whiskers and a coiled body, displays powerful hind limbs and a forked, curled tail. Around them are S-shaped cloud patterns.

The archer's ring was worn on the left or right thumb to draw a bowstring in ancient China. It also served decorative and symbolic purposes in later periods. Starting from the mid-Warring States period, as archery became less relevant to rituals, jade archer's rings gradually declined but developed as decorative pieces.

西汉（前 206 年—8 年）

玉

长 7.30 厘米，宽 4.00 厘米

上海博物馆

Western Han (206 BCE – 8 CE)

Jade

L. 7.30 cm, W. 4.00 cm

Shanghai Museum

75 | ## 绿釉陶博山炉
Boshan Lu (hill-shaped censer)

炉盖呈山峰状，豆形炉身，炉柄中部饰三周凹弦纹，炉盘方圆唇，平折沿，敞口，斜曲浅腹，底心中空与炉柄相连。此炉炉盖与炉身相接，并不具使用意义。粉褐色胎，胎质较粗，施墨绿色釉，釉面莹润，底心及边缘未施釉。

博山炉属熏炉，是熏香时使用的香具。炉盖群山仿海上仙山而作，是汉代神仙方士信仰的反映。出现于西汉中期，其渊源可上溯至战国时期的豆形熏炉。西汉中期炉以青铜材质为主，陶质为辅。西汉晚期，博山炉的使用范围进一步扩展，同时部分墓葬中开始出现炉盖并不镂空的博山炉，属专为随葬而用的明器。东汉时期，博山炉以釉陶为主，主要作为丧葬明器使用，此件绿釉博山炉为东汉中晚期的典型产品。

The lid of this censer resembles a mountain peak, while the body of the burner is shaped like a *dou* (food vessel). The middle part of the handle is decorated with three groove lines. The incense plate has a trimmed lip, a flat folded rim, an open mouth, and a slightly curved shallow belly, with its bottom connected to the handle, hollow at the center. The lid is attached to the body and doesn't serve any functional purpose. The censer features a brownish-grey body with a coarse texture, covered in dark green glaze, giving it a glossy finish. The base with its edges is left unglazed.

The *boshan lu* belongs to the category of incense burners. The design of the lid, resembling legendary sacred mountains rising from the sea, reflects Daoist beliefs during the Han dynasty. These censers first appeared in the mid-Western Han period, with their origins tracing back to *dou*-shaped censers from the Warring States period. During the mid-Western Han, they were primarily made of bronze, with some crafted from earthenware. In the late Western Han period, *boshan lu* began appearing as burial items, some with non-perforated lids, indicating their use purely for burial. In the Eastern Han period, glazed earthenware *boshan lu* became more prevalent, mainly serving as burial items. This green-glazed one is a representative example from the mid to late Eastern Han period.

汉（前 206 年—220 年）

陶

通高 12.70 厘米，盘径 15.70 厘米，底径 10.80 厘米

上海博物馆

倪汉克先生捐赠

Han (206 BCE – 220 CE)

Green-glazed earthenware

Overall H. 12.70 cm, plate dia. 15.70 cm, base dia. 10.80 cm

Shanghai Museum

Gift of Mr. Henk Nieuwenhuys

76 | 玉刚卯

Gangmao (rectangular amulet)

白玉。玉刚卯是辟鬼驱疫，压制邪祟的佩玉，四面刻有"正月刚卯（既央），灵殳四方"等三十余字辟邪韵文。刚卯流行于两汉，一说与汉代皇室的刘（劉）姓可拆字为"卯金刀"有关，有尊重国姓及强刘之意。东汉有制规定，凡着朝服必佩刚卯，玉质刚卯仅列侯以上者方可佩戴。

汉代"辟邪厌胜"之风极盛，"厌胜"意为"厌而胜之"，源于原始巫术，旨在压制邪祟。除玉刚卯、玉严卯外，玉器中还有玉翁仲、玉司南佩等具辟邪驱疫、趋吉纳福等特殊含义的佩饰。

This white jade *gangmao* is an amulet believed to ward off evil spirits and diseases. It is engraved on all four sides with a protective charm consisting of more than thirty characters. The *gangmao* was popular during the Han dynasty. Its name is supposed to be derived from the surname Liu (劉) of the Han royal family, the character of which can be separated into parts of 卯 (*mao*), 金 (*jin*), and 刀 (*dao*), symbolizing reverence for the royal surname and the idea of strengthening the Liu's powen. During the Eastern Han period, regulations stipulated that *gangmao* was a compulsory accessory for court attire, and only marquises and higher-ranking officials were allowed to wear jade ones.

In the Han dynasty, there was a prevailing belief in exorcism rooted in ancient shamanistic practices. Apart from jade amulets like *gangmao* and *yanmao*, various other jade ornaments such as figures of Ran Wengzhong and *sinan* (compass)-shaped pedants were created with symbolism of protection against evil and seeking good fortune.

东汉（25 年—220 年）

玉

宽 1.05 厘米，高 2.10 厘米

上海博物馆

Eastern Han (25–220)

Jade

W. 1.05 cm, H. 2.10 cm

Shanghai Museum

77 | 玉严卯

Yanmao (rectangular amulet)

东汉（25 年—220 年）

玉

长 1.00 厘米，高 2.10 厘米

1993 年出土于上海市黄浦区打浦桥顾叙墓

上海博物馆

Eastern Han (25–220)

Jade

L. 1.00 cm, H. 2.10 cm

Excavated from the tomb of Gu Xu at Dapuqiao,

Huangpu District, Shanghai, in 1993

Shanghai Museum

白玉。四面刻有韵文："疾日严卯，帝令夔化。慎而固伏，化兹灵殳。既正既直，既觚既方。庶疫刚瘅，莫我敢当。"玉严卯与玉刚卯韵文内容有所不同，两者并称"双印"，皆具"护身"之意。

This white jade *yanmao* is engraved on all four sides with a protective charm. The text on *yanmao* differs from that on *gangmao*. These two types of amulets are jointly referred to as "the seal duo", both protecting the wearer.

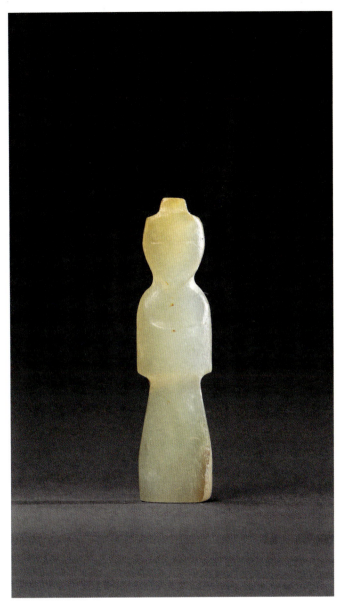 

78 | 玉翁仲
Wengzhong (amuletic figure)

青玉。相传翁仲是秦始皇时期震慑匈奴、镇守庙宇的勇士，而后演化成为人们心中镇邪驱魔的守护神，以铜、石雕像常见。玉翁仲腰部多有穿孔，以供穿系，随身佩戴以驱邪逐魅。

This amulet of green jade depicts the figure of Ran Wengzhong, a warrior believed to deter the Xiongnu and protect temples from the time of Qin Shi Huang (reigned 221–210 BCE). Later, Wengzhong became a symbolic guardian that wards off evil, often depicted in bronze or stone statues. Many jade figures of Wengzhong have a hole at the waist for wearing and carrying as amulets against malevolent forces.

东汉（25 年—220 年）
玉
长 3.20 厘米，宽 0.70 厘米
上海博物馆

Eastern Han (25–220)

Jade

L. 3.20 cm, W. 0.70 cm

Shanghai Museum

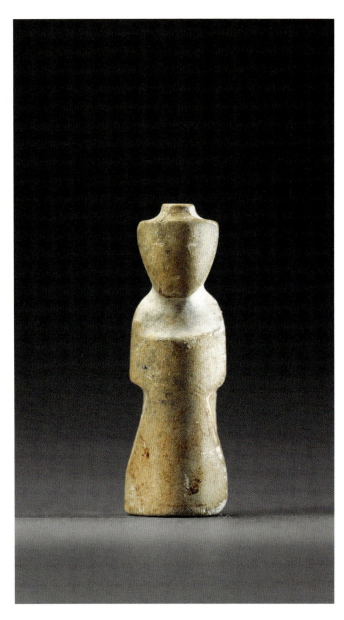

79 | 玉翁仲
Wengzhong (amuletic figure)

东汉（25 年—220 年）

玉

长 2.80 厘米，宽 0.90 厘米

上海博物馆

Eastern Han (25–220)

Jade

L. 2.80 cm, W. 0.90 cm

Shanghai Museum

青玉，灰白色沁。玉翁仲多施刀简洁，面部仅以三五阴刻线琢眼、口，颈部和腰下施以撤刀法，粗犷有力，以三角形斜平面突出头部、身体的轮廓。

This green jade figure of Wengzhong has greyish-white alterations. The figure's features are carved with simplicity, with only three or five incised lines for the eyes and mouth. The neck and lower waist are treated with the beveling carving technique in bold and powerful lines. The head and body contours are highlighted by triangular slanting surfaces.

80 | 玉司南佩
Sinan (compass)-shaped Pendant

黄玉，局部有灰黄色沁。于工字型佩顶端仿司南之形。"司南"本是中国古代利用磁场制成的指南仪器，在汉代占卜之风盛行时成为测算凶吉的工具。玉司南佩主要流行于东汉，随身佩戴以辟邪压胜。

东汉（25 年—220 年）
玉
长 3.30 厘米，宽 1.30 厘米，高 2.00 厘米
上海博物馆

Eastern Han (25–220)
Jade
L. 3.30 cm, W. 1.30 cm, H. 2.00 cm
Shanghai Museum

This piece of yellow jade has greyish-yellow alterations. The top of the dumbbell-shaped pendant features a design of *sinan*, which was originally an ancient Chinese compass. During the Han dynasty when divination was popular, the *sinan* became a tool for predicting good and bad luck. Jade *sinan*-shaped pendants were popular mainly in the Eastern Han, and people wore them as amulets to ward off evil.

81 | 玉买地券

Land-sale Contract

碧玉。买地券是古代以地契形式置于墓中的随葬品，既是冥间墓冢的凭证，又是敬告土地神灵以免受干扰的通报文书，源于西汉，盛于东汉。此件买地券为迄今发现的唯一玉质作品，双面均阴刻隶体铭文，大意为公元81年墓主靡婴购得这块墓地，并记录了东南西北四方广幅及见证人。

This piece made of green jade belongs to the "land-sale contracts" as burial items in ancient China. It served as both evidence of ownership of the tomb in the underworld and written notice to the land gods to prevent disturbances. Such practice originated in the Western Han and prevailed during the Eastern Han. This particular piece is the only known jade contract of its kind. The inscriptions in clerical script on both sides indicate that in 81 CE, Mi Ying, the deceased and tomb owner, purchased this burial plot. The text also records its fictional size and witnesses.

东汉（25 年—220 年）

玉

长 7.30 厘米，宽 4.60 厘米

上海博物馆

Eastern Han (25–220)

Jade

L. 7.30 cm, W. 4.60 cm

Shanghai Museum

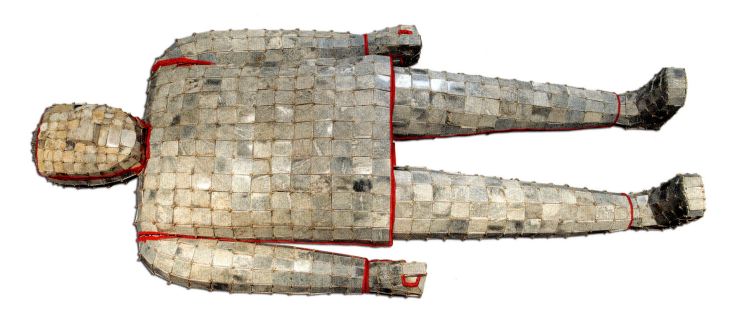

82 | 金缕玉衣
Jade Burial Suit Threaded with Gold Wire

一般认为，玉衣是由周代的缀玉面幕和缀玉衣服发展而来。汉代成为皇帝和高级贵族的殓尸用具，用金属丝将玉片连缀而成，是我国最具特色的丧葬用玉。玉衣又名"玉柙""玉匣"。汉代玉衣有金缕玉衣、银缕玉衣、铜缕玉衣和丝缕玉衣等，依身份地位不同而缕质各异，西汉时尚未形成严格的等级制度。但从目前西汉楚国墓葬出土资料看，只有楚王或王后死后用金缕玉衣，王国内其他王室成员和高级贵族死后使用银缕玉衣、玉衣套或玉面罩，表现出了较明显的等级差别。东汉时期对玉衣的使用实行严格的等级制度，《后汉书·礼仪志》中有较为详细的记载。曹魏黄初三年（222）魏文帝曹丕作《终制》禁止使用玉衣。

It is generally believed that jade suits originated from burial face coverings or garments sewn with jade pieces from the Zhou dynasty (1046-256 BCE). During the Han dynasty, suits made by connecting jade pieces with metal wires have become burial items exclusively for emperors and high-ranking nobles. They are regarded as the most distinctive jade burial item of ancient China. In the Han dynasty, different types of jade suits emerged, categorized by the use of gold wire, silver wire, copper wire, or silk thread, depending on the deceased's status. While the Western Han did not yet set a system for jade suits, findings from Chu State tombs suggest a notable hierarchy. Only the Chu kings and queens were buried in gold-wired jade suits, while other members of the royal family and high-ranking nobles wore silver-wired jade suits, jade covers, or jade face covers. The use of jade suits started to be strictly regulated during the Eastern Han, as recorded in the *Book of Later Han*. In 22 CE, Emperor Wen of the Wei State, Cao Pi, issued a law to ban the jade suits.

汉（前 206 年—220 年）

金、玉

长 168.00 厘米，肩宽 68.00 厘米

徐州博物馆

Han (206 BCE – 220 CE)

Gold and jade

L. 168.00 cm, shoulder W. 68.00 cm

Xuzhou Museum

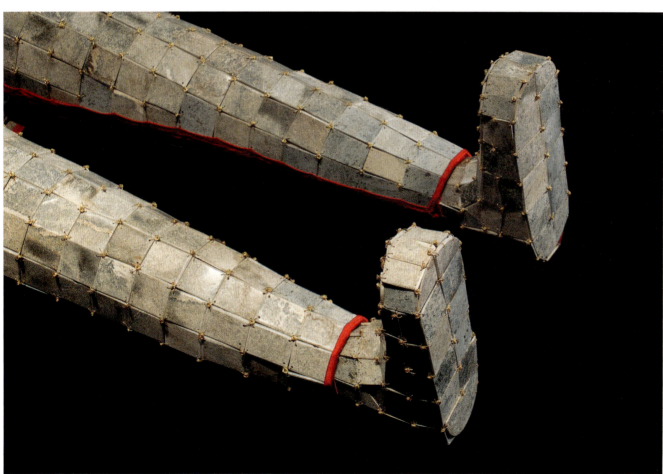

83 蒲纹玉璧
Bi (disc) with Woven Pattern

青白玉，局部有赭褐色沁。玉璧外圈及内孔边缘均阴刻轮廓线，玉璧两面纹饰相同，均按三个方向的平行线碾琢，留下类似蜂巢的蒲纹装饰。蒲纹主要流行于战国至西汉中期，在玉璧、玉环等玉器中常见。

汉代厚葬之风盛行，葬玉的使用规模远超以往。具有一定等级的汉代墓葬中多出土有玉璧，分布于墓主身体上下及头、脚部周围等多个位置，反映了汉代先民希冀以玉通灵保尸体不腐，或能通天以助墓主灵魂升天成仙的愿望。

This disc of greenish-white jade, with reddish-brown alterations, is engraved with incised lines on its outer rim and hole edge. Both sides of the disc bear identical woven patterns, resembling honeycombs, in parallel lines in three directions. This pattern was popular during the Warring States and the mid-Western Han period and is commonly found in jade artifacts like discs and rings.

The Han dynasty saw a prevalent trend of lavish burials, leading to an unprecedent increase in the use of burial jades. Jade discs were frequently unearthed from Han dynasty tombs of high-ranking individuals, scattered around the deceased's head, feet, and other body parts. This practice reflects the people's wish to use jade as a means to preserve the body from decay and to assist the soul in its pursuit of immortality.

西汉（前 206 年—8 年）

玉

径 14.00 厘米，内径 4.00 厘米，厚 0.20 厘米

上海博物馆

Western Han (206 BCE – 8 CE)

Jade

Dia. 14.00 cm, inner dia. 4.00 cm, thickness. 0.20 cm

Shanghai Museum

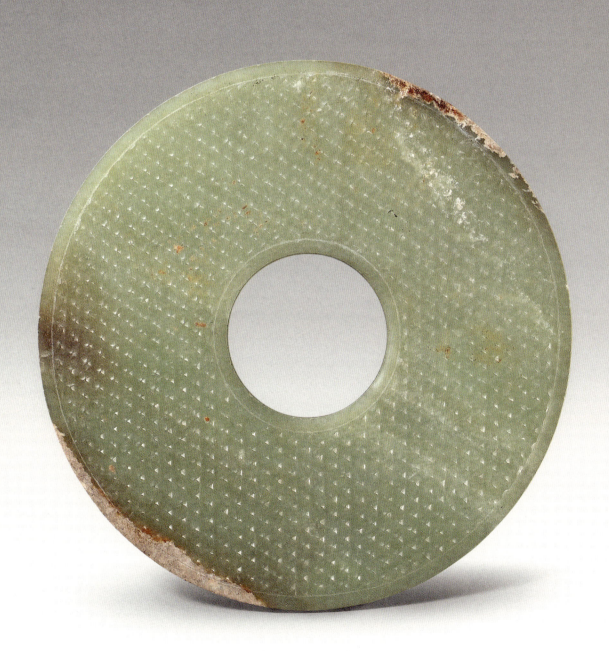

84 | **蝉形玉琀**
Cicada-shaped *Han* (mouthpiece)

青白玉。玉琀是置于死者口中的葬玉，早在新石器时期，就有因不忍逝者空其口而塞入米、粱、贝、珠、玉等物的葬俗。汉代常以蝉作琀，有借蝉脱壳寄寓复活再生的祈愿。

此件蝉形玉琀是"汉八刀"技艺的典型代表。"汉八刀"是汉代典型玉雕技法之一，一指刀工简练，寥寥数刀而就；二指用刀讲究，左右对称，奏刀后槽线对称若"八"字。

This greenish-white jade cicada is a burial jade placed in the mouth of the deceased. As far back as the Neolithic period, there was a custom of placing items such as rice, grains, shells, pearls, and jade in the mouth of the deceased to symbolize offerings and sustenance. During the Han dynasty, jade mouthpieces were often shaped in cicadas, embodying the wish for rebirth and reincarnation symbolized by the cicada's molting.

This jade cicada is a quintessential example of the "Han Eight Cuts" (*Han ba dao*) technique, one of the typical jade carving techniques from the Han dynasty, characterized by the masterful use of knives. The number "eight" here refers to both the concision of cuts, accomplished within just a few strokes, and the elegantly symmetrical groove lines that resemble the Chinese character 八 for "eight".

东汉（25 年—220 年）
玉
长 6.70 厘米，最宽 3.40 厘米
上海博物馆

Eastern Han (25–220)
Jade
L. 6.70 cm, max. W. 3.40 cm
Shanghai Museum

85 │ 玉枕

Headrest

西汉（前 206 年—8 年）

玉

长 28.70 厘米，宽 9.50 厘米，高 8.50 厘米

1996 年出土于徐州火山刘和墓

徐州博物馆

Western Han (206 BCE – 8 CE)

Jade

L. 28.70 cm, W. 9.50 cm, H. 8.50 cm

Excavated from the tomb of Liu He at Huoshan,

Xuzhou, in 1996

Xuzhou Museum

枕面与前后两侧各镶贴有三组玉片，并以金箔切条贴在玉片上组成菱形及三角形图案，枕面中间一块玉片呈青白色，抛光极为平滑，一侧并有圆润的抹角。枕周边以金箔包边，玉片的拼缝处也贴有金箔。

The top, front, and back sides of the headrest feature three sets of jade pieces meticulously inlaid, which are adorned with gold foil strips to form diamond and triangular patterns. In the center of the top is a greenish-white jade piece, polished to a remarkably smooth finish, with one side bearing a rounded edge. The borders and seams of the headrest are all trimmed with gold foil.

上海博物馆『百物看中国』文物艺术出境大展系列

CHINA 100: Outbound Exhibition Series of Arts and Cultures

86 | 缀玉面饰
Face Covering

面罩以多种形状的玉片组成，玉片为青灰色或灰白色。多有褐色杂斑，正面抛光，玉片角均穿孔，用于装缀。耳部下有四个小玉环，直径 1.3 厘米。整件玉面罩共用玉片三十片，其中一片为后配片。

覆盖死者面部的面罩起源较早，古籍中有瞑目、布巾、覆面之说，考古发现的实物可以追溯到西周时期，当时的玉面罩即较为写实。汉代玉面罩延续了早期写实缀玉的传统，同时又有所创新，形成了与玉枕、窍塞和握玉的完整组合。

This face covering is composed of jade pieces in various shapes, typically in greenish-grey or greyish-white hues with brown mottling. The front is polished, and the corners of the jade pieces are pierced for attachment. Below the ears are four small jade rings, each with a diameter of 1.3 cm. The entire covering consists of thirty jade pieces, one of which is a replacement piece.

The use of face coverings for the deceased has an ancient origin, as mentioned in historical texts. Archaeological findings trace this tradition back to the Western Zhou period, where the jade face coverings of that era were realistic in appearance. During the Han dynasty, the tradition of using jade face coverings continued, following the earlier realistic style while also introducing innovations that led to a cohesive ensemble, including jade headrests, plugs, and grips.

西汉（前 206 年—8 年）

玉

长 22.50 厘米，宽 24.50 厘米，厚 0.20 厘米

1991 年出土于徐州后楼山汉墓

徐州博物馆

Western Han (206 BCE – 8 CE)

Jade

L. 22.50 cm, W. 24.50 cm, thickness 0.20 cm

Excavated from a Han tomb at Houloushan, Xuzhou, in 1991

Xuzhou Museum

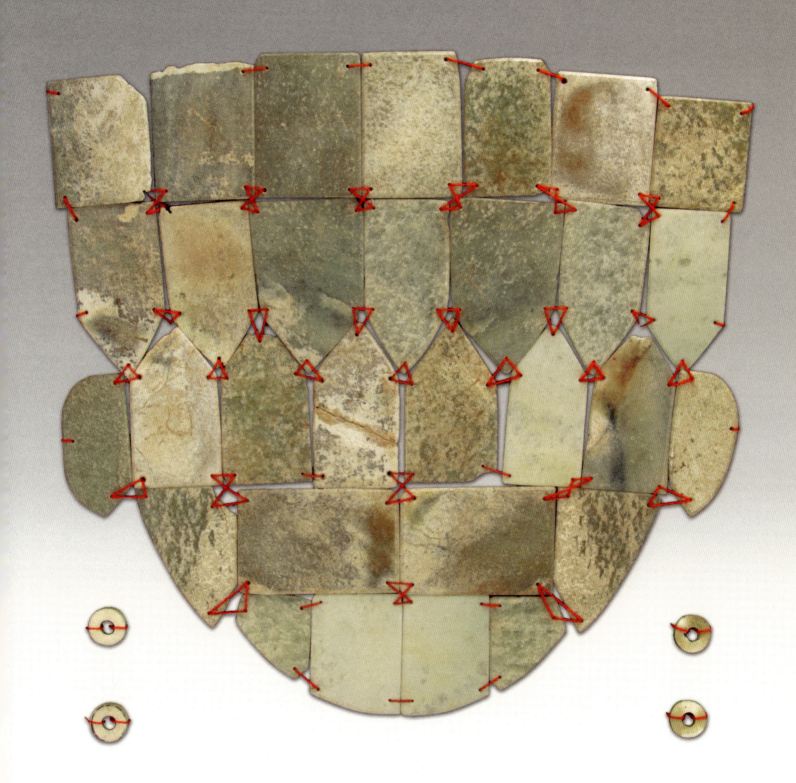

87 | 玉眼盖
Eye Coverings

西汉（前 206 年—8 年）

玉

长 1.90 厘米，宽 1.30 厘米，高 0.20 厘米

2006 年出土于徐州奎山 M11

徐州博物馆

Western Han (206 BCE – 8 CE)

Jade

L. 1.90 cm, W. 1.30 cm, Thickness 0.20 cm

Excavated from Tomb M11 at Kuishan, Xuzhou, in 2006

Xuzhou Museum

　　此玉眼盖石化程度较重，上下均钻孔，应是穿缀使用。所谓"九窍"系指人体的口、双眼、双耳、双鼻孔、肛门和生殖器等。两汉时期丧葬用玉盛行，人们对形魄的保护更加重视，相信"金玉在九窍，则死者为之不朽"，便在死者身体各窍塞（盖）玉，是丧葬用玉中很重要的组成部分。

This pair of jade eye coverings is heavily petrified. Each piece has holes for attachment both on top and bottom. The term "nine orifices" refers to the body's mouth, two eyes, two ears, two nostrils, anus, and genitals. During the Han dynasty, jade was widely used in burial. Preserving the deceased's physical form was a matter of great concern, and gold and jade placed in the nine orifices were believed to protect the body from decay. Therefore, jade pieces were inserted into or put over these orifices, which became a significant aspect of burial jade.

88 | 玉瑱
Tian (ear plugs)

西汉（前 206 年—8 年）

玉

（1）长 2.10 厘米，宽 0.90 厘米，高 0.90 厘米

（2）长 2.10 厘米，宽 0.90 厘米，高 0.90 厘米

2006 年出土于徐州奎山 M11

徐州博物馆

Western Han (206 BCE – 8 CE)

Jade

(1) L. 2.10 cm, W. 0.90 cm, H. 0.90 cm

(2) L. 2.10 cm, W. 0.90 cm, H. 0.90 cm

Excavated from Tomb M11 at Kuishan, Xuzhou, in 2006

Xuzhou Museum

此玉瑱为塞耳葬玉。青玉，基本呈圆柱状，上窄下宽，截面呈椭圆形。

This pair of jade tian was used as ear plugs in burial. Both are made of green jade and are basically cylindrical, tapering from top to bottom, with an oval cross-section.

89 | 玉鼻塞
Nose Plugs

西汉（前 206 年—8 年）

玉

（1）长 2.50 厘米，宽 0.90 厘米

（2）长 2.40 厘米，宽 0.60 厘米

2008 年出土于徐州小长山四号墓

徐州博物馆

Western Han (206 BCE – 8 CE)

Jade

(1) L. 2.50 cm, W. 0.90 cm

(2) L. 2.40 cm, W. 0.60 cm

Excavated from Tomb M4 at Xiaochangshan,

Xuzhou, in 2008

Xuzhou Museum

此玉鼻塞为塞鼻孔葬玉。青玉，表面有沁蚀，略微泛白，呈长条柱形状。边棱经过打磨，截面近方形。

This pair of jade nose plugs is burial jade for blocking the nostrils. Both are made of green jade, with white alterations on the surface, and take the form of elongated rectangular prisms. The edges are polished, and the cross-section is nearly square.

90 | 玉蝉
Cicada

西汉（前 206 年—8 年）

玉

长 4.00 厘米，宽 2.50 厘米

2006 年出土于徐州奎山 M11

徐州博物馆

Western Han (206 BCE – 8 CE)

Jade

L. 4.00 cm, W. 2.50 cm

Excavated from Tomb M11 at Kuishan, Xuzhou, in 2006

Xuzhou Museum

此玉蝉为琀蝉，体较宽，底部平。头部外弧凸起，颈部饰斜线纹。背拱，上饰云纹。双翅并拢，翼上纹络清晰。尾部外弧，微上翘。整体较为写实，刻画精细，栩栩如生。

This jade cicada is a *han* (mouthpiece) with a wide body and a flat bottom. Its head has a raised arc edge, and the thorax bears diagonal lines. The back arches, adorned with cloud patterns. Clear venation fills the folded wings. The abdomen ends with a curve and slightly tilts upward. This cicada is quite realistic, finely detailed, and lifelike in its depiction.

91 | 玉握
Pig-shaped *Wo* (grips)

西汉早期的握玉一般是玉璜，然而西汉中期以后大部分的握玉就演变成了玉猪。猪在古代是财富的象征，玉握做成猪形，象征死者握有财富。西汉的玉握猪在风格上基本属于写实造型，采用阴刻和浮雕相结合的手法，线条简练，形象逼真，琢磨光滑，在玉料的选取上一般不太讲究，多为随地取材。前期体型一般比较修长，而后期开始变为厚壮，圆雕感增强。

In the early Western Han period, the typical form of jade grips was the *huang* (arc-shaped pendant). However, from the mid-Western Han period onwards, most jade grips turned into jade pigs. Pigs symbolized wealth in ancient China. So pig-shaped grips imply that the deceased grabbed the wealth. Those from the Western Han generally come in a realistic style, combining incising and relief carving techniques. The lines were concise, the imagery lifelike, and the surface smooth. They were often made from local materials, not particular about the jade quality. The pigs first appeared to be generally slender, while in later periods, they became thicker and more three-dimensional.

西汉（前 206 年—8 年）

玉

长 9.30 厘米，宽 2.40 厘米，高 3.10 厘米

1996 年出土于徐州火山刘和墓

徐州博物馆

Western Han (206 BCE – 8 CE)

Jade

L. 9.30 cm, W. 2.40 cm, H. 3.10 cm

Excavated from the tomb of Liu He at Huoshan,

Xuzhou, in 1996

Xuzhou Museum

上海博物馆『百物看中国』文物艺术出境大展系列

CHINA 100: Outbound Exhibition Series of Arts and Cultures

92 | **绿釉陶望楼**

Watch Tower

　　陶楼分三层，一层四壁开拱门；二层四壁开窗，平坐四面饰卧棂栏杆，四角各立一执弩武士俑；三层四壁开窗，平坐四面饰卧棂栏杆，立二执弩武士俑于对角处，楼顶为庑殿式，屋面饰瓦垄。外施绿釉，内部中空露胎处呈粉红色。

　　东汉时期庄园经济空前发展，豪强地主在庄园内设坞壁、武库以及武装人员，用以防卫、守护庄园在动乱岁月中不受外界侵扰，成为割据一方的地方性武装。此件望楼之中的武士俑持弩警戒，军事性质明显，是对当时庄园经济的真实反映。

This earthenware tower includes three stories. The first story has four open arched doorways. The second features four windows, and balustrades with horizontal lattice adorn the four sides of the terrace. In each corner stands a warrior figurine holding a crossbow. The third story shares the same structure as the second, with two crossbow archers standing in diagonal corners. The rooftop is in a *wu-dian* (five-ridged hip roof) style with tile ridges. The entire tower is coated with green glaze on the exterior, while the exposed body on the inside reveals a pinkish hue.

During the Eastern Han, the manorial economy saw unprecedented growth. Wealthy landlords built up ramparts and armories with armed personnel within their manors to defend their properties against external threats during turbulent times, becoming local armed forces. The warrior figurines within this tower, positioned as sentinels with crossbows, clearly display the military feature of manorialism during that era.

东汉（25 年—220 年）

陶

高 51.00 厘米，每边长 22.70 厘米

上海博物馆

Eastern Han (25–220)

Green-glazed earthenware

H. 51.00 cm, side L. 22.70 cm

Shanghai Museum

上海博物馆『百物看中国』文物艺术出境大展系列

CHINA 100: Outbound Exhibition Series of Arts and Cultures

93 | 陶屋
House

汉（前 206 年—220 年）
陶
高 20.00 厘米，纵 23.20 厘米，横 27.00 厘米
1953 年出土于广州市东郊龙山岗出土
上海博物馆

Han (206 BCE – 220 CE)
Earthenware
H. 20.00 cm, L. 23.20 cm, W. 27.00 cm
Excavated from Longshangang, Guangzhou, in 1953
Shanghai Museum

陶屋表现的是一种院落的形式，平面呈"L"型的房屋，与同样呈"L"型的围墙，组成了一个长方形的院落。房屋分成两间，正房屋后有门，另有门与一侧厢房相通，形成了客厅与卧房功能性的分隔。院落与房子都有可供狗进出的狗洞。一种以单个家庭组成的建筑，是当时平民生活的最真实的反映。

This earthenware depicts an L-shaped house with walls of the same shape, forming a rectangular courtyard. The house is divided into two rooms. The main room has a door at the rear, while another door connects it to a side room, which functionally separates the living room and the bedroom. Both the courtyard and the house have dog holes. This type of building, representing a single-family household, is the most authentic reflection of the commoners' life during that time.

94 | 绿釉陶磨房
Millhouse

陶磨房是通体施铅绿釉的低温陶器，为建筑模型，多为陪葬用的明器。磨房设在一个长方形院落中，后半部设有屋顶，并有一人正在工作，这应该是一处以人力为主的磨房，中国磨房常见的动力有畜力、水力和人力。磨房内有碓臼与石磨各一具，这是常见的加工粮食的用具，碓臼是用重力来粉碎粮食，而石磨则是碾磨。以小麦为主的北方和以稻谷为主的南方，都需要这两种工具来加工粮食。磨房的出现是中国耕作农业高度发展后出现的，它也是中国社会分工更加细化、专门化的结果，同时磨房的存在也是人们集聚生活的需要，直至现在的中国农村，磨房也往往是一个村落或一个集镇的中心所在。

This millhouse is a low-fired earthenware lead-glazed in green, a model made for burial. The millhouse is situated in a rectangular courtyard, with a roof covering the rear half. The figurine of a worker suggests that it represents a millhouse primarily powered by human labor. In ancient China, mills relied on animal power, hydropower, or human power. Inside the millhouse, there is a mortar and pestle for grain crushing through gravity and a stone mill for grinding. These tools were crucial for processing grains, whether wheat in the north or rice in the south. The emergence of millhouses was driven by the significant developments in agricultural cultivation in China, reflecting the increasing specialization and division of labor in society. Millhouses were also important places where people gathered. Even today, in rural China, millhouses often serve as a central hub for a village or town.

汉（前 206 年—220 年）

陶

高 15.00 厘米，长 26.40 厘米，宽 19.80 厘米

上海博物馆

Han (206 BCE – 220 CE)

Green-glazed earthenware

H. 15.00 cm, L. 26.40 cm, W. 19.80 cm

Shanghai Museum

上海博物馆『百物看中国』文物艺术出境大展系列

CHINA 100: Outbound Exhibition Series of Arts and Cultures

95 | 绿釉陶溷

Hun (pig toilet)

溷，意为带猪圈的厕所。陶胎，通体施铅绿釉，为墓葬模型明器，整体分上、下两层。下层为长方形围墙，一侧墙外有阶梯，可通上层厕所。厕上之屋，则名溷轩，为悬山顶，方形门，开小窗，厕内底部有长方形孔，下通猪圈。

圈内有一绿釉陶猪，形象写实逼真，是汉代墓葬中常见的厕所与养猪积肥相结合的模型。除猪以外，饲养马、牛、羊的厩、牢、圈都不和厕所在一起。

汉代的建筑实物，至今存留在地面上的除几座石阙、石室外，人们所能看到的比较形象的资料，应该只有建筑明器了，它们较为直观地表现了古代建筑物的形制和构造，反映了一定的社会生活习俗。

The term *hun* means a toilet mounted over a pigsty. This green lead-grazed earthenware is a model made for burial. It consists of two stories: the lower story features a rectangular wall, with a staircase on one side that leads to the privy on the upper floor. The privy, known as *hunxuan*, has a gable roof, a square door, and small windows. A rectangular hole at the bottom connects to the pigsty.

Inside the pigsty is a green-glazed earthenware pig, realistically depicted. This type of pig toilet model is commonly found in Han dynasty burials. Unlike pigsties, enclosures for other animals, including stables, cowsheds, and sheepfolds, were not located together with toilets.

Besides a few tangible remains of stone towers and chambers, these architectural models as burial items are the only informative sources of Han dynasty architecture that have survived to this day. They provide a clear representation of the ancient architectural styles and structures, revealing related social customs and practices.

汉（前 206 年—220 年）

陶

高 15.10 厘米，长 20.40 厘米，宽 18.60 厘米

上海博物馆

Han (206 BCE – 220 CE)

Green-glazed earthenware

H. 15.10 cm, L. 20.40 cm, W. 18.60 cm

Shanghai Museum

96 | 绿釉陶夔龙纹囷
Qun (granary) with Dragon

盖与器身一体。伞形盖，盖顶开圆孔，盖面斜直，其上饰瓦垄。筒形腹，平底，三兽足。腹部饰三组弦纹，每组弦纹间模印纹饰。除足端及外底部分区域外，通体施绿釉，足端露胎处呈粉红色。

囷是古代储粮设施，《说文解字》载："囷，廪之圜者，从禾在囗中。"作为模型明器的陶囷出现于春秋中期陕西咸阳、陇县地区的秦墓中，并在汉代逐渐流行至全国范围。汉代陶囷造型丰富、种类多样，此型陶囷主要流行于关中地区。

The roof is integrated with the body of the granary, taking on an umbrella shape with a circular opening at the top and tile ridges on the sloping surface. The body is cylindrical with a flat bottom and three animal-shaped feet. Three sets of string patterns adorn the body, alternating with molded dragon patterns. The entire model is glazed in green, except for the feet and certain parts of the exterior bottom, where the clay displays a pinkish hue.

The term *qun* refers to ancient grain storage facilities. According to the *Shuowen Jiezi* (*An Explicetion of Written Characters*) dictionary, the *qun* is a circular granary, with the character 囷 comprising 禾 (grains) enclosed within 囗 (an enclosure). Earthenware models of granaries, used as burial items, were found in Qin tombs from the mid-Spring and Autumn period in the Xianyang and Longxian regions of Shaanxi. They gradually spread across the country during the Han dynasty in various shapes and types. This particular type of granary model was prevalent in the Guanzhong region.

汉（前 206 年—220 年）

陶

高 27.60 厘米，囷面径 20.90 厘米

上海博物馆

Han (206 BCE – 220 CE)

Green-glazed earthenware

H. 27.60 cm, roof dia. 20.90 cm

Shanghai Museum

97 | 绿釉陶井
Well

陶胎，通体施铅绿釉。为随葬模型明器，造型精美，写实生动，极富生活气息。

井，作为人们生活饮水的重要设施，早在新石器时代便已出现。后也用来灌溉农田，普遍用于生产与生活当中。陶井的原型来自于现实生活中的水井，因各地自然环境的差异，水井带有较强的地域特征，陶井则凸显了这一特征。

从已有的考古发现来看，两汉墓葬中出土的陶井，一般由井身、井栏、井架、井亭、地台、附属设施（如汲水罐、陶水斗、滑轮、水槽）等组成。根据有无井身可以分为两大类型，这两类又可以进一步划分为不同的地区类型，它们有着各自不同的分布区域及流行年代。

This green lead-glazed earthenware well is a finely crafted burial model with vivid design, evoking a sense of daily life.

Wells, as crucial facilities for drinking water supply, have been in use since the Neolithic period in ancient China. They later functioned for irrigation, essential for both production and everyday use. Earthenware wells are modeled after real water wells. Due to regional variations in natural environments, the wells exhibit distinct regional characteristics, which are highlighted in these earthenware representations.

Based on archaeological findings, the earthenware wells unearthed from Han dynasty tombs typically consist of several components, including the wellhead, railings, frames, roof, platform, and ancillary utensils like pots, buckets, pulleys, and sinks. Wells can be categorized into two main types based on the presence of a wellhead, and either has regional variations with distinct distribution areas and periods of popularity.

汉（前 206 年—220 年）

陶

高 48.60 厘米，底径 17.50 厘米

上海博物馆

Han (206 BCE – 220 CE)

Green-glazed earthenware

H. 48.60 cm, base dia. 17.50 cm

Shanghai Museum

98 | ## 绿釉陶水塘
Pond

圆盘形水塘，盘沿及塘中塑水鸭、游鱼，姿态各异，生动活泼。底部以外通体施绿釉。

汉代六畜养殖发展迅速，各地官吏如颍州太守黄霸、渤海太守龚遂、不其县令僮种等均大力提倡人们养殖家畜、家禽，从其提倡的养殖数量看，一般一家一户养一两只猪、四五只鸡等，各地墓葬出土家畜家禽，也可见一定的规律性，常见猪一、狗一、鸡二的组合，另有牛、羊、鸭、鹅、龟、鱼等各类。从出土陶俑组合看，鸭、鹅类水禽在北方地区的出土数量不如南方。

此类陶制圈养水禽模型，在东汉较为流行，结合四川大邑安仁镇出土渔猎水鸭图，可以窥见汉代养殖、捕食水禽的情况，其饮食及物质丰富，由此可见一斑。

This circular model of a water pond is adorned with sculptures of ducks and swimming fish along the rim and inside the pond, displaying diverse and lively postures. The entire exterior is coated with green glaze, except for the bottom.

During the Han dynasty, livestock and poultry husbandry saw rapid development, promoted by many local officials. Based on the quantities suggested by these officials, it was common for households to raise one or two pigs and four or five chickens. Archaeological findings of livestock and poultry models in tombs from different regions also reflect the typical combination of one pig, one dog, and two chickens, with additional cattle, sheep, ducks, geese, turtles, and fish. It is noticeable that the unearthed waterfowl models like ducks and geese are less in the north than in the south.

Models of domestic waterfowl like this earthenware were popular during the Eastern Han period. Echoing the hunting and fishing scene relief found in Anrenzhen of Dayi, Sichuan, it provides insights into waterfowl raising and hunting during the Han dynasty, suggesting the abundant food sources in that era.

汉（前 206 年—220 年）

陶

宽 31.50 厘米，盘高 4.70 厘米，底径 22.20 厘米

上海博物馆

倪汉克先生捐赠

Han (206 BCE – 220 CE)

Green-glazed earthenware

W. 31.50 cm, plate H. 4.70 cm, base dia. 22.20 cm

Shanghai Museum

Gift of Mr. Henk Nieuwenhuys

99 绿釉陶烧烤炉
Roaster

折沿，深腹，平底，底部有长方形漏灰孔数道。下承四足，为熊形。炉上架有两枚烤签，签上各置四只蝉。通体施绿釉，釉面略有返铅现象。陕西历史博物馆也藏有一件类似的绿釉陶烤炉，其形制与样式几乎与本器物一致。

汉代的烹饪技法中除去蒸、煮、煎等，烧烤也颇为流行。在汉代画像石上常出现烧烤的画面，如山东诸城凉台汉墓出土的"庖厨"画像，就有厨师在方形烤炉前烤肉串的形象。除去常规的肉类炙烤，汉代也有烤蝉、食蝉的习惯。曹植的《蝉赋》属于汉晋时期流行的咏物赋，其中描写蝉的悲惨命运时提到："委厥体于膳夫，归炎炭而就燔。"表明当时以烧烤的方式烹饪蝉是一件极为平常的事情。

This earthenware roaster features a folded rim, a deep belly, a flat bottom, and several rectangular holes at the bottom. It is supported by four bear-shaped feet. The roaster has two barbeque skewers on it, each holding four cicadas. The entire surface is coated in a green glaze, with a slight silver sheen caused by corrosion deposits. The Shaanxi History Museum also houses a green-glazed roaster, which shares almost identical form and style with this one.

During the Han dynasty, in addition to steaming, boiling, and frying, roasting was a popular cooking method. Scenes of roasting are often depicted in Han dynasty stone reliefs. For example, the kitchen relief unearthed from the Han tomb in Liangtai of Zhucheng, Shandong, shows a chef grilling meat skewers on a square roaster. There was also a custom of roasting and consuming cicadas during the Han dynasty. Cao Zhi (192–232), a prince of the Wei state, wrote the *Ode to the Cicada*, which belongs to the prevalent object-description poems from the Han to the Jin (266–420). The poem mentions that the cicadas "have their body handed over to the chef to be roasted over a red-hot charcoal fire", which suggests that roasting cicadas was common during that time.

汉（前 206 年—220 年）

陶

长 23.80 厘米，盘宽 15.60 厘米，高 8.30 厘米

上海博物馆

倪汉克先生捐赠

Han (206 BCE – 220 CE)

Green-glazed earthenware

L. 23.80 cm, roaster W. 15.60 cm, H. 8.30 cm

Shanghai Museum

Gift of Mr. Henk Nieuwenhuys

汉（前 206 年—220 年）

陶

通高 23.90 厘米，纵 39.70 厘米，横 30.70 厘米，

釜高 8.50 厘米，釜口径 18.60 厘米

上海博物馆

Han (206 BCE – 220 CE)

Green-glazed earthenware

Overall H. 23.90 cm, L. 39.70 cm, W. 30.70 cm

Caldron H. 8.50 cm, mouth dia. 18.60 cm

Shanghai Museum

100 绿釉陶印纹单眼灶
Single Burner Stove

　　红陶胎，通体施低温绿釉。整个陶灶由灶和釜两部分组成。单眼灶呈马蹄形，模制，整个灶及灶上所附属的烹饪肉食、炊具全是一模脱出。灶面火眼左侧盛盘中有龟、鸭、猪、鱼，旁边放置钩、刀、竹筐、葫芦瓢等工具。右侧印有"用此灶葬者后世子孙富贵长乐未央……"多字。靠近烟囱处刻划一条大鱼。在陶灶有限的空间里表现出丰富多彩的物质生活，可见设计之巧妙。

　　汉代以釜、甑蒸饭，而不再用鬲、甑合体之甗；这是由于炉、灶的普及，使三足器在蒸煮用具中退居次要地位之故。汉代对灶很重视，西汉中期以后的大墓中，以陶灶随葬之风很流行，各地出土陶灶的形制略有不同。

This model consists of the stove and the caldron, made of red clay coated with low-fired green glaze. The arch-shaped stove, together with the food and utensils on it, are all molded in one piece. On the left side of the burner is carved with dishes of turtle, duck, pig, and fish, along with tools like hooks, knives, bamboo baskets, and gourd ladles. On the right side, there is an inscription that promises wealth and happiness to the deceased's descendants. A large fish is carved beside the chimney. Within the very limited space, the ingenious design vividly portrays a rich material life.

During the Han dynasty, due to the widespread use of stoves, tripod cookware that was put directly over a fire gave way to *fu* (caldrons) and *zeng* (steamer pots) vessels which were more commonly used to steam food. Stoves were valued during the Han dynasty, and it became a popular trend starting from the mid-Western Han period to include earthenware stove models as burial items in large tombs. The forms of these stoves vary slightly across regions.

101

陶灶
Stove

灶体前方后圆，呈马蹄形，灶面有火眼两个，模印钩、帚、瓢、铲等炊具，另有圆盘、方案等，案上可见如鱼等食物。灶前出有遮烟沿，长方形灶门，灶门一侧为烧火人，另一侧有瓶，灶不封底。灰陶质地，不施釉。

西汉陶灶以素面居多，最初只有单火眼，随时代发展，火眼增至三到四个，并增加各类装饰。汉代陶灶上的器具丰富，主要有炊具、餐具及食品三类。炊具有勺、瓢、帚、叉、箅等，餐具有盘、碗、耳杯、筷等，食物以鱼、鳖最为多见，其次是鸡、鸭、猪头、牛腿等，从中可以窥见汉代的饮食及器用组合。更为有趣的是，各地区出土陶灶的器物组合有所差异，如耳杯是汉代常见酒具，常在陶灶中成对出现，但在关中地区较为少见，与食肉有关的叉等，在甘肃、宁夏地区最为多见。北方地区陶灶出土时，火眼上往往置釜、甑等炊具，南方地区除釜、甑外，往往在前部的火眼上置双耳锅，广州的陶灶还常在灶台两侧附装汤缶，是为地域特色，而本件陶灶，在关中一带最为流行。

The arch-shaped stove has two burners on the top, with stamped hooks, brooms, ladles, shovels, and other kitchen utensils, as well as dishes and trays with food like fish. The front of the stove has a smoke baffle and a rectangular door with a stoker on one side and a bottle on the other side. The bottom of the stove is left unenclosed. The entire piece is made of grey earthenware and not glazed.

Most earthenware stoves from the Western Han have plain surfaces and a single burner. Only in later periods, models with three to four burners and various decorations began to appear. The items found on Han dynasty stove models have a rich range and mainly belong to three categories: cookware, tableware, and food. Cookware includes hooks, ladles, brooms, forks, and steamer racks; tableware includes plates, bowls, ear cups, and chopsticks. The most found food items are fish and turtles, followed by chickens, ducks, pig heads, and beef legs. These combinations reveal the dietary habits and utensils used during the Han dynasty. Interestingly, the composition of items on unearthed stove models varies across regions. For example, ear cups, as ordinary wine vessels in the Han dynasty that often appear in pairs on stoves, are less common in the Guanzhong region. Tools for eating meat, such as forks, are more prevalent in Gansu and Ningxia in the north-west. In northern regions, stove models are often found with caldrons and steamers on the burners, while in southern regions, additional double-handled pots are frequently placed on the front burners. In Guangzhou, the stoves often have soup pots attached to both sides of the stove. All these differences highlight the stoves with distinct regional features. This particular type of stove model prevailed in the Guanzhong region.

汉（前 206 年—220 年）

陶

长 21.00 厘米，宽 16.00 厘米，高 7.80 厘米

上海博物馆

倪汉克先生捐赠

Han (206 BCE – 220 CE)

Earthenware

L. 21.00 cm, W. 16.00 cm, H. 7.80 cm

Shanghai Museum

Gift of Mr. Henk Nieuwenhuys

102 彩绘陶女俑

Figurine

此器为侍女俑，袖手直立，衣裾及地，行不露足。

汉代出土的各类彩陶，其身着的各类服饰是研究中国古代服饰的重要资料。

在中国历史上，服饰是政治的一部分，其重要性远超出服装在现代社会的地位，是君王施政的重要制度之一。

公元前 221 年秦始皇建国后，为巩固统一，相继建立了各项制度，包括衣冠服制，统一了服装、旗帜的颜色。而完整的冠服制度则在汉朝得到了确立。到了东汉明帝永平二年（59 年），揉合秦制与三代古制，重新制定了祭祀服制与朝服制度，冕冠、衣裳、鞋履、佩绶等各有严格的等级差别，从此汉代服制得到了确立。服装成为一种身份地位的象征，一种符号，它代表个人的政治地位和社会地位，使人人恪守本分，不得僭越。

This figurine of a female servant stands upright with her hands folded, her robe flowing all the way to the floor, concealing her feet.

The various unearthed painted earthenware figurines from the Han dynasty provide valuable views into ancient Chinese clothing. Clothing was an integral part of governance in ancient China, holding greater importance than in modern society. Regulations regarding attire were part of the ruling systems.

After the founding of the Qin dynasty in 221 BCE by Qin Shi Huang (reigned 221–210 BCE), who sought to consolidate his rule, all kinds of systems were adopted, including regulations on clothing colors. The comprehensive clothing system further developed during the Han dynasty. In 59 CE, the hierarchy of ceremonial and court attire was restored by combining the rules of the Qin dynasty and earlier traditions. It encompassed aspects like headwear, clothes, footwear, and accessories, each with strict hierarchical distinctions, marking the official establishment of the Han dynasty system. Clothing became an indicator of one's social and political status, emphasizing the importance of adhering to one's duty and not exceeding it.

西汉（前 206 年—8 年）

陶

高 37.60 厘米，宽 13.50 厘米

上海博物馆

Western Han (206 BCE – 8 CE)

Painted earthenware

H. 37.60 cm, W. 13.50 cm

Shanghai Museum

103 彩绘陶女俑

Figurine

女俑拱手肃立，足蹬平头履，身着深衣，腰系束带，交领右衽，领口很低，露出里衣的衣领，为三重衣。

深衣是汉代最为普遍的服饰，并对中国后世服饰产生过重要的影响，在中国古代服装史上占有重要地位。其本身上衣下裳相连、被体深邃，款式多样，适用范围广，上至王公贵族，下至平民百姓均可适用，裁剪方便、工艺成熟，有着很高的实用价值。另一方面，深衣又体现了中国传统思想，是展现我国古代风俗、文化、人物的重要载体。

深衣在魏、晋之后虽然不再流行，但魏晋时期的大袖长衫、隋唐时期的宽袍、唐代的袍下加襕及后来的质孙服、腰线袄子、宋代的衫、元代的长袍、明代的补服都是这种上衣下裳相连的深衣制的发展演变，甚至于近代的旗袍、现代的连衣裙、日本的和服以及韩国的韩服从一定的意义上来讲，都是受了深衣形制的启示而发展演变而来的，由此可见深衣的影响久长深远。

This female figurine stands with folded hands, wearing *shenyi* ("the deep garment"), flat-headed shoes, and a tied waist sash. The *shenyi* has a crossover right lapel with a low collar that reveals the inner garments, showing a three-layered outfit.

The *shenyi* was the mainstream clothing in the Han dynasty, leaving a significant impact on subsequent Chinese clothing. It includes upper and lower parts sewn together to wrap the body deep within cloth. There were diverse styles that served the needs of all classes, from nobles to commoners. It was simple in cut and construction, making it highly practical. At the same time, the *shenyi* shows profound cultural significance as a display of ideas, customs, and historical figures of ancient China.

Although the *shenyi* fell out of fashion after the Wei and Jin dynasties, the influence of its connected upper-and-lower structure can be seen in the evolving styles of clothing in later periods. To name a few: the broad-sleeved robe of the Wei and Jin period, the loose robe of the Sui and Tang dynasties, the robe with lower hem of the Tang dynasty, the *zhisun* (a single-colored robe) and the *yaoxian'aozi* (a plait-line robe) of the Yuan dynasty, the shirt of the Song dynasty, and the *bufu* (an official's robe) of the Ming dynasty. The *shenyi* exerted influences even on modern *qipao*, one-piece dresses, Japanese kimono, and Korean hanbok.

汉（前 206 年—220 年）

陶

连木座高 61.20 厘米，宽 17.00 厘米

上海博物馆

Han (206 BCE – 220 CE)

Painted earthenware

H. (with wooden base) 61.20 cm, W. 17.00 cm

Shanghai Museum

中国古代事死如生。印信作为个人重要代表信物，是最重要的殉葬品之一，有时会使用木印替代实用印信入葬，也有实用铜印、玉印入葬。内容包括个人姓名、字、号，曾任官名等。

Ancient Chinese treated death as an extension of life. Seals as significant personal emblems were among the most important burial items. They can be bronze or jade seals or sometimes wooden replicas. The inscriptions might include the deceased's name, courtesy name, style name, or official title.

104 "中私府长李封字君游" 铜印

Seal with Inscription "Zhong Si Fu Zhang Li Feng Zi Jun You"

新莽（9年—23年）
铜
纵 2.35 厘米，横 2.35 厘米，高 2.10 厘米
上海博物馆

Xin (9–23 CE)
Bronze
L. 2.35 cm, W. 2.35 cm, H. 2.10 cm
Shanghai Museum

这件"中私府长李封字君游"铜印有着新莽时期的典型形制。以龟为钮，表明着主人的身份并不普通。新莽时期的龟钮与其他时代的龟钮形态并不一样，它有着鲜明的时代特征：龟首略伸，平视前方，龟背有着饱满的曲线，背甲纹理清晰，四肢健硕有力。印面文字线条曲直相谐，端庄大方。一般的印章印面文字为四字，内容也比较单一，这方印印面文字内容丰富，包含有印主的职官（中私府长）、个人姓（李）、名（封）、字（君游）四种信息，是这个时代新创。

This bronze seal exhibits the typical form of the Xin period. The turtle-shaped knob indicates the owner's distinguished status. The turtle knob of the Xin period differs in form from those of other eras, displaying distinct characteristics: the turtle's head slightly extends, facing forward, and its back curves highly with clear shell patterns, while its limbs are robust. The legend is elegantly composed with curved and straight lines. Unlike most seals, which typically bear four-character inscriptions with little content, this seal contains rich information, including the owner's official position (*Zhongsifu zhang* 中私府长, an official managing the empress's finances), surname (Li 李), given name (Feng 封), and courtesy name (Junyou 君游). Such a combination of personal information was innovative for the era.

105 | "魏嫽" 玉印
Seal with Inscription "Wei Liao"

　　玉材的获取本就不易，精工制作更为难得。玉质个人用印一般只能在高等级的墓葬中发现，是个人身份地位的象征。

　　这枚"魏嫽"印玉质精美，印面文字线条的每个细节处理得极其到位，文字造型刚柔相济，制作工艺精湛。作为一件艺术品，它在中国印章史上有着重要地位，是汉代玉印的经典之作。

The acquisition of jade was not easy in ancient China, and jade artifacts with meticulous craftsmanship were even rarer. Jade personal seals were only found in the tombs of high-ranking individuals, indicating the deceased's social status.

This jade seal displays fine quality, with every detail on the inscription skillfully executed. The characters balance strength and softness, showcasing exceptional craftsmanship. As an artwork, it holds a significant position in the history of Chinese seals, representing a classic example of Han dynasty jade seals.

东汉（25 年—220 年）

玉

纵 2.35 厘米，横 2.35 厘米，高 1.70 厘米

上海博物馆

Eastern Han (25–220)

Jade

L. 2.35 cm, W. 2.35 cm, H. 1.70 cm

Shanghai Museum

上海博物馆『百物看中国』文物艺术出境大展系列

CHINA 100: Outbound Exhibition Series of Arts and Cultures

106

"赵莽私印章" 铜印
Seal with Inscription "Zhao Mang Si Yin Zhang"

此印是东汉时期私人用印。印体残存着包裹印章的织品，表明印章主人对它的珍视。它一般佩戴在墓主人的腰际，以便取用。此印印面用了一种中国特有的文字：鸟虫书。这是一种以汉字为主体框架，将鸟虫形象高度概括后，装饰在汉字笔画之上，是一种工艺性极强的书体，盛行在两汉时期。

This is a private seal from the Eastern Han period. The remnants of fabric on it indicate how the owner cherished and wrapped it. Private seals were typically worn at the waist of the tomb owner for easy access. This seal's inscription is in a distinctive Chinese script, the "bird-worm script", which is known for the abstract depictions of birds and worms decorating the characters' strokes. It is a highly artistic script that was popular during the Han dynasty.

东汉（25 年—220 年）
铜
纵 2.40 厘米，横 2.50 厘米，高 2.35 厘米
上海博物馆

Eastern Han (25–220)
Bronze
L. 2.40 cm, W. 2.50 cm, H. 2.35 cm
Shanghai Museum

107

"常宫印·常直君" 两面木印
Double-legend Seal with Inscriptions "Chang Gong Yin" and "Chang Zhi Jun"

此为东汉两面穿带木印。以木为印是汉代随葬印中常用的方式，但因难以保存，故数量极为稀少。此印保存完好，因木质收缩略有变形。

This is a double-legend wooden seal from the Eastern Han period. The wooden seals were commonly used for burials in the Han dynasty, but only a few have survived to this day. This seal is well-preserved despite slight deformation due to the natural contraction of the wood.

东汉（25 年—220 年）
木
纵 1.20 厘米，横 1.40 厘米，高 0.89 厘米
上海博物馆

Eastern Han (25–220)
Wood
L. 1.20 cm, W. 1.40 cm, H. 0.89 cm
Shanghai Museum

108 | 陶狗
Dog

东汉（25 年—220 年）

陶

长 24.90 厘米，宽 10.80 厘米，高 22.20 厘米

2006 年出土于成都东林四组汉墓

成都文物考古研究院

Eastern Han (25–220)

Earthenware

L. 24.90 cm, W. 10.80 cm, H. 22.20 cm

Excavated from the Han-dynasty tombs at Group No.4
of Donglin Community, Chengdu, in 2006

Chengdu Institute of Archaeology

出土于成都东林四组东汉时期砖室墓中。泥质红陶。呈站立状，昂首挺胸，两耳竖起，尾部卷曲，颈部与腹部有红色背带交结于背部。汉代饲养犬类一般用来看家护院、田猎、娱乐和食用等，墓葬中随葬陶狗的情况也十分普遍。

This red earthenware dog was unearthed from an Eastern Han brick-chamber tomb in Group No.4 of Donglin Community, Chengdu. It stands proudly with its head held high, ears perked up, and tail curled. A red strap crosses from the neck to the belly and is fastened on the back. During the Han dynasty, dogs were raised for guarding home, hunting, entertainment, and meat, and it was quite common to put earthenware dogs alongside the deceased in tombs.

109 | 绿釉陶狗
Dog

陶狗四足站立，昂首耸耳，尾部蜷曲，通体施铅绿釉，有宽带绕颈至背结环，可见为驯养之犬。

汉代养犬之风极盛，朝廷设有狗监，专司养犬，汉武帝甚至建有"犬台宫"。上有所好，下必甚焉，社会各阶层亦热衷驯养，据《礼记·少仪》记载，犬分为守犬、田犬及食犬。守犬是看家护院之犬，田犬为田猎所用，食犬则供人宰杀食用。此外，亦可用于祭祀及斗狗娱乐。汉代有着事死如生的丧葬观念，讲求厚葬，墓室型制和结构尽量模仿活人住宅，随葬品方面，也尽量做到应有尽有，几乎包括生人衣、食、住、行等各方面。墓葬中陶狗的普遍出土，正是当时社会对狗大量需求的反映。

This green lead-glazed earthenware dog stands tall with its head held high, ears perked up, and tail curled. It has a strap crossed around its neck and fastened at the back, indicating domestication.

Keeping dogs was highly popular during the Han dynasty. The imperial court had a dog care position, and Emperor Wu of Han (156–87 BCE) even constructed a "Dog Palace" for dog fighting. This enthusiasm for dogs was widespread across society. According to the *Book of Rites*, dogs were categorized into guard dogs, hunting dogs, and meat dogs. Additionally, dogs appeared in sacrificial ceremonies and entertainments, such as dog fighting. The Han dynasty was passionate about lavish burials. The tomb structures and styles sought to replicate the dwelling of the deceased, and the burial items covered all aspects of everyday life. The frequent presence of earthenware dogs in tombs reflects the prevailing trend of raising dogs during that time.

东汉（25 年—220 年）
陶
长 39.00 厘米，高 32.00 厘米
上海博物馆

Eastern Han (25–220)
Green-glazed earthenware
L. 39.00 cm, H. 32.00 cm
Shanghai Museum

110 | 绿釉陶鸡

Rooster

昂首，尾部高高翘起，足部被简化成圈足状。以模具制成，可见明显的合模痕迹。虽然工艺较为简单，但雄鸡的形象极为生动。施绿釉，泛银色，施釉不及底。由于铅绿釉易于受到水和大气的溶蚀，形成沉积物。当沉积物达到一定厚度时，受光线的影响就会产生银白色的光泽。

陶鸡在汉墓中极为常见，见有雄鸡、雌鸡和子母鸡三种类型。汉代的养鸡技术和管理非常成熟。刘向的《列仙传》有这样一则故事："祝鸡翁，洛人也，居尸乡北山，养鸡百余年，鸡有千余头，皆立名字，暮栖树上，昼则散之，欲引，呼名即依呼而至，卖鸡及子得千余万。"虽是志怪故事，但也从侧面反应了汉代养鸡业的成熟。

This rooster stands with its head held high and tail raised. The shape of its feet is simplified into a circular base, and the traces of mold seams suggests that it was made through molding. Despite simplicity, the representation of the rooster is remarkably lifelike. The entire surface, except for the bottom, is coated in green lead glaze, giving off a silver sheen caused by the accumulation of corrosion deposits.

Earthenware chickens were frequently encountered in Han dynasty tombs, including roosters, hens, and hen-and-chick types. During the Han dynasty, chicken farming techniques and management reached an advanced level. The *Biographies of Immortals* compiled by Western Han historian Liu Xiang (77–6 BCE) includes a tale about Zhujiweng, who had raised chickens for over a century. He farmed more than a thousand chickens that would perch on trees at night, roam freely during the day, and respond when called by their names. Zhujiweng earned millions of coins from selling these chickens. While this is a legendary tale, it sheds light on the development of chicken farming during the Han dynasty.

汉（前 206 年—220 年）

陶

高 16.70 厘米，长 20.10 厘米

上海博物馆

Eastern Han (25–220)

Green-glazed earthenware

H. 16.70 cm, L. 20.10 cm

Shanghai Museum

111 | 陶卧羊

Couchant Ram

　　羊首微含，前足向后弯曲，卧于地上，身下有底座。虽然是一件简单的随葬品，但体态丰腴，卧姿及神态极为生动，体现出匠人良好的造型能力。汉代的养羊业极为发达，根据《史记·货殖列传》中的记载有羊二百五十只以上的人，其每年收入等于一个"千户侯"。另外，汉阳陵的陪葬坑和大臣陪葬墓中曾出土了数百件陶羊。

The ram has a slightly inclined head, with its front legs bent backward, crouching on the base beneath it. Although it is an ordinary burial object, its plump shape, couchant posture, and facial expression are vivid, demonstrating excellent modeling skills. Sheep farming saw significant development during the Han dynasty. As recorded in the *Records of the Grand Historian*, individuals with over 250 sheep could earn an annual income equivalent to that of a "Marquis of a Thousand Households". Hundreds of earthenware sheep were unearthed from the accompanying pits and tombs of high-ranking officials in Yangling, the imperial mausoleum of Emperor Jing of Han (188–141 BCE).

汉（前 206 年—220 年）

陶

高 9.10 厘米，长 12.70 厘米

上海博物馆

Han (206 BCE – 220 CE)

Earthenware

H. 9.10 cm, L. 12.70 cm

Shanghai Museum

112 | 陶鸭
Duck

立姿，造型生动，身上的羽毛清晰可见，足部虽然被简化，但亦抓住了鸭掌的特征。鸭在汉代已经成为常见的家禽。从陶鸭的出土情况来看，至汉代，全国绝大部分地区都已有了家鸭的分布。不过由于鸭子喜水，南方的养殖或较北方发达。陶鸭的出土情况也能反映这些，河南等地区的陶鸭以站姿为主，数量相对较小。而两广地区，陶鸭的形态各异，数量亦多于北方地区。

This earthenware duck stands upright with a lively and detailed appearance, and the feathers on its body are clearly visible. The feet are depicted in a simplified manner yet still show the characteristics of the webbed feet. Ducks were already common domestic fowl during the Han dynasty. Archaeological findings of earthenware ducks suggest that by the Han dynasty, ducks were distributed throughout most parts of the country, while duck farming was more developed in the southern regions, the abundant waters of which were inhabitable for waterfowl. In central regions like Henan, fewer duck models have been unearthed, with most in a standing posture. In contrast, in the southern regions like Guangdong and Guangxi, duck models exhibit diverse forms, with quantities surpassing those in the north.

汉（前 206 年—220 年）

陶

高 16.50 厘米，长 20.30 厘米

上海博物馆

Han (206 BCE – 220 CE)

Earthenware

H. 16.50 cm, L. 20.30 cm

Shanghai Museum

主办单位 Organizers

上海博物馆 Shanghai Museum

徐州博物馆 Xuzhou Museum

成都文物考古研究院 Chengdu Institute of Archaeology

总策划 General Curators

上海博物馆 Shanghai Museum：褚晓波 Chu Xiaobo

徐州博物馆 Shanghai Museum：李晓军 Li Xiaojun

成都文物考古研究院 Chengdu Institute of Archaeology：颜劲松 Yan Jinsong

展览策划 Exhibition Curators

陈杰 Chen Jie　谷娴子 Gu Xianzi

内容统筹 Content Curators

施远 Shi Yuan　王樾 Wang Yue　彭涛 Peng Tao　宗时珍 Zong Shizhen

展览协调 Exhibition Coordination

徐立艺 Xu Liyi　徐泽诚 Xu Zecheng　向敏瑄 Xiang Minxuan

图版说明（按姓氏拼音首字母排序）Authors of Entries

上海博物馆 Shanghai Museum

陈洁 Chen Jie　冯泽洲 Feng Zezhou　高义夫 Gao Yifu　华慈祥 Hua Cixiang　孔品屏 Kong Pinping　师若予 Shi Ruoyu
王樾 Wang Yue　张亚莉 Zhang Yali　郑昕雨 Zheng Xinyu　周成慧 Zhou Chenghui　周浩 Zhou Hao

徐州博物馆 Xuzhou Museum
缪华 Miao Hua　仇文华 Qiu Wenhua

成都文物考古研究院 Chengdu Institute of Archaeology
李佩 Li Pei

图版摄影 Photography

上海博物馆 Shanghai Museum：薛皓冰 Xue Haobing　朱琳 Zhu Lin　张旭东 Zhang Xudong　陆铖 Lu Cheng

成都文物考古研究院 Chengdu Institute of Archaeology：唐文武 Tang Wenwu

徐州博物馆 Xuzhou Museum

英文翻译 Translation

徐泽诚 Xu Zecheng　向敏瑄 Xiang Minxuan

翻译审校 Translation Revision

徐立艺 Xu Liyi　徐泽诚 Xu Zecheng

特别支持 Special Support

佰路得信息技术（上海）有限公司

BACK & ROSTA LTD.

版权申明 Copyright Declaration

图书在版编目(CIP)数据

不朽的玉甲 : 中国汉代文物精品 / 上海博物馆编
. -- 上海 : 上海书画出版社, 2023.12
ISBN 978-7-5479-3258-2

Ⅰ. ①不… Ⅱ. ①上… Ⅲ. ①文物–中国–汉代–图
录 Ⅳ. ①K871.412

中国国家版本馆CIP数据核字(2023)第245979号

上海博物馆"百物看中国"文物艺术出境大展系列

不朽的玉甲：中国汉代文物精品

上海博物馆 编

主　　编	褚晓波
责任编辑	王　彬　吕　尘
特约编辑	张思宇　丁唯涵
审　　读	雍　琦
特约编审	陈　凌
装帧设计	汪　超　王贝妮
图文制作	包卫刚
美术编辑	盛　况
技术编辑	包赛明
印装监制	朱国范

出版发行	上 海 世 纪 出 版 集 团　上海书画出版社
地　　址	上海市闵行区号景路159弄A座4楼
邮政编码	201101
网　　址	www.shshuhua.com
E－mail	shuhua@shshuhua.com
设计制作	上海维翰艺术设计有限公司
印　　刷	上海中华商务联合印刷有限公司
经　　销	各地新华书店
开　　本	635×965 1/8
印　　张	26
版　　次	2023年12月第1版　2023年12月第1次印刷

书　号	ISBN 978-7-5479-3258-2
定　价	280.00元

若有印刷、装订质量问题，请与承印厂联系